Strands of Memory Revisited

Sweet and Bittersweet Memories and
Meditations

William R. Tracey, Ed.D.

iUniverse, Inc.
New York   Bloomington

Strands of Memory Revisited
Sweet and Bittersweet Memories and Meditations

This is a work of fiction. All of the characters, names, incidents, organizations, and dialogue in this novel are either the products of the author's imagination or are used fictitiously.

iUniverse books may be ordered through booksellers or by contacting:

iUniverse
1663 Liberty Drive
Bloomington, IN 47403
www.iuniverse.com
1-800-Authors (1-800-288-4677)

Because of the dynamic nature of the Internet, any Web addresses or links contained in this book may have changed since publication and may no longer be valid. The views expressed in this work are solely those of the author and do not necessarily reflect the views of the publisher, and the publisher hereby disclaims any responsibility for them.

ISBN: 978-1-4401-1062-7 (sc)
ISBN: 978-1-4401-1063-4 (ebook)

Library of Congress Control Number: 2008942767

Printed in the United States of America

iUniverse rev. date: 2/19/2009

Cover design by Deborah Beaudoin

Dedication

My Wife
Kathleen Lucille (Doheny) Tracey

My Children
William Raymond Tracey, Jr.
Kevin Thomas Tracey
Brian John Tracey
Kathleen Lucille Bastille
Maura Gail Tarbania
Sean Michael Tracey

My Grandchildren
Tama Lee Letellier Lumpkin
Jacqueline Marie Munson
Michele Marie Coffman
Sean Keenan Letellier
Laine Tracey Tarbania
William Raymond Tracey III
Timothy Patrick Tracey
Kathleen Elizabeth Tracey
Victor Carrillo Tracey
Kolby Lynne Tracey
Kaylyn Michelle Tracey
Siara Carrillo Tracey

My Great Grandchildren
Kaila Lee Lumpkin
Grace Marie Munson

My Friend and Companion
Else-Marie Birgit Bowe

Listen to these words
They are the songs of my life
Store them in your heart

Contents

Living on the Cape
There's no other place like it
Excepting Heaven

Foreword

This is a collection of verse, mainly but not exclusively blank verse, written over the past decade or so. I have no illusions about the quality of the verse. Some of it is insightful, some pedantic, and some mundane. Some of it is reasonably good poetry; some is mediocre. Nonetheless, all of it comes from my heart. And I make no apologies for that.

I don't believe that my children, grandchildren, and great grandchildren know that I'm an incurable romantic with strong emotions. My wife, Kathleen, knew it and used that knowledge to my advantage. I was honored and elated to be her husband, lover, and friend for more than 53 years. She truly understood me and loved me despite the fact that I was and am a flawed man.

I love being loved. I have always needed someone to love me simply because I was deprived of much love for many years. Although my foster mother, Josephine, tried valiantly to meet that need by providing affection and emotional support during my troubled childhood and adolescence, she was not completely successful. However, she was my first rescuer. And my wife was the second. In more recent years my friends, and later, my children, and still later, a companion and friend, filled that need and role.

So. many of the verses were written for Kathleen Lucille Tracey, my late spouse, lover, friend, and supporter for 56 years. Others were written for my children, grandchildren, great grandchildren, in-laws, and friends. Still others were simply my ruminations and cerebrations about life, the nature that surrounds us, or the things that befall us mortals. I must also admit that I began to write verse simply because I was lonely and didn't have anyone else close enough frequently enough to talk with and share my feelings.

Poetry gave me a chance to create listeners and say what I desperately needed to say without feeling guilty about it. So I did exactly that.

I also know that these verses reveal more about William Raymond (O'Neill) Tracey than most men would want to have exposed to the view of others, particularly the members of their family. But, I have always been a realist. I want my progeny to know the real person that I am — my dreams, my fantasies, my weaknesses, my naiveté. So, there are very few things about me that remain hidden, and those are withheld only because I believe that they would be hurtful to others if revealed.

All of the verse in this volume commemorates people who were very important in my life. Their love, friendship, support, courage, and strength have been an inspiration and a blessing to me. This verse is my way of memorializing them and sharing them with each other and the world.

Putting my emotions into words and allowing my loved ones to experience with me the things that troubled, hurt, pleased, or delighted me, helped me to heal and made my life more meaningful and rewarding. Being able to express myself through the written word and to share my thoughts and feelings with others are true blessings.

I hope and pray that the people to whom this volume is dedicated will remember me with forbearance and love — and also in their prayers. I also hope that they and those they love will enjoy good health, happiness, and all of the things that will be useful to them in the plan of God

With deepest love to you all,
William R. (O'Neill) Tracey

Family

Money means little
Family is everything
Never forget that

Our Collage of Cultures

Our family exemplifies the "melting pot"
metaphor for America.
Representing five of six continents.
only Australia is not among them
Our countries of origin include
Canada, United States, Columbia,
Venezuela, Ireland, Spain, Portugal, France,
Switzerland, Finland, Poland, Italy, China,
and other countries in Africa
the Balkans, and the Middle East.
Our nationalities: American Indian,
Canadian French, Irish, Polish, Columbian,
Spanish, Portuguese,
Native South American, Finnish, Swiss,
Italian, Jewish, Chinese, and African American.
My offspring are in my prayers
in a warm and special way
today, tomorrow, and all days.
That's my promise!

My Special Gift

Throughout my life I've received
many gifts that I hold dear.
Those blessings include
the people who loved me and are no longer here —
my parents, foster parents, and parents-in-law,
my wife of more than 53 years
and my four sisters and three brothers,

But, the greatest gift I have received
in all my days
is the one great gift made up of separate parts,
every one an individual gift
and each one securely resting in my heart.
This is the gift that has made my life complete,
and at every thought of that beneficence,
my heart skips a beat.

That gift is one that God sent to me
— one that is perfect and uniquely mine.
It is my family: my six children,
twelve grandchildren,
and two great grandchildren —

blessings that God has given to me.
But, for whatever the reason,
and known only to God and not to me,

There is one element of that gift
that has been closest to me —
one who must go nameless.
For to diminish in any way
my love for any of the others
would be tactless and unpardonable.
And I hope that my relationships
with all of the others
would allow every one of them
to say with complete certainty,
"That's me."

Our Family

God made us a family.
We work together and play together.
We need each other and love each other.
So, we ask the Lord to bless the family we love
and comfort us each day.
As daytime turns into nighttime,
please bring us peace, we pray.
When morning becomes tomorrow,
let all our cares be small.
and guide us with your wisdom.
Lord bless us one and all. Amen.

My Special Gardens

I have three beautiful gardens
That blossom and thrive inside me.
The first contains two lovely daisies
And four handsome carnations
That I treasure with all my heart.
They are the best gifts God has given me
Ones that I would never exchange for anything
My six children, my precious offspring,
Two girls, Kathleen and Maura, and four boys.
Bill. Jr., Kevin, Brian, and Sean.
They are the first garden of my life.

My second garden contains eight lovely daisies
And four handsome carnations,
Grandchildren that mean the world to me,
Eight girls, Tamra, Jackie, Mikie, Laine,
Kathleen, Kolby, Kaylyn, and Siara,
And four boys. Sean, L.B., Tim, and Victor.

My third garden is not yet complete
For it contains only two gardenias.
Two girl great grandchildren. Kaila and Grace.
And with time and God's beneficence,
There are more blossoms to come.

I'll be with all of my gardens until God takes me.
They are now the reason for my existence,
The incentive for my everyday life.
Every day I feed and water my plants
So they can grow straight and healthy.
I do that by daily prayer.

Thoughts, Wishes, and Prayers
for My Grandchildren

Here are my beliefs about the most important things in life:
Have realistic, achievable, and worthwhile goals.
Find your real talents, the things you like and do best.
Everyone has one or more; the challenge is to identify them.
Commit to learning, mastering, and burnishing
the skills and knowledge needed
to make the most of those talents.
Be persistent in the pursuit of your goals.
Never be satisfied that you have achieved perfection.
Work at the job without tiring or yielding to adversity.

Always remember the importance of family —
revere your ancestors on both sides of your family,
your parents and grandparents, siblings, aunts and uncles, and
cousins —their talents, accomplishments,
and the rich heritage
they have left to you or now share with you.
Love them for what and who they are or were
and show them that you love them.

Here are my wishes for you:
That you find and exploit your God-given talents.
That you honor your heritage and your family.

And finally, here are my prayers for you:
That you have a long, healthy, happy, and rewarding life.
That you find a true soul mate
and together have healthy and happy children.
That you always exemplify the values of
love of God and compassion and charitableness toward all
others.

My Foster Mother

A precious gift when I needed someone
who cared for and about me,
someone I didn't knowingly search for
but one who found me by the unhappy circumstance
of my mother's deathbed wish for her sister's help
which, by God's grace, became a blessing for both of us.
That was my Mom!

That event gave her the child she had always wanted
and me a caring mother and normal childhood
made all the sweeter and rewarding to me
because the results were so unexpected —
the fulfillment of dreams not experienced before
of happiness, contentment, and fulfillment galore.
That was my Mom!

She was thoughtful, determined, and indomitable,
considerate, prudent, solicitous, and focused.
Unschooled but bright, clever, quick-witted.
and with an insatiable appetite for learning.
An avid reader, a questioning mind, and
a true supporter of quality education.
That was my Mom!

She was buoyant, cheerful, sprightly, and upbeat,
caring, attentive, observant, and protective.
warm, amiable, genial, and openhearted.
feminine, affectionate, and loving.
That was my Mom!

Always open-hearted; never harsh or cynical
Occasionally resolute but never intractable.
Always thoughtful but never arrogant

Never impulsive and invariably dependable.
Unconventionally authentic, and relentlessly purposeful.
At times precise and exacting, but invariably accessible.
That was my Mom!

She was family oriented — family was first in importance
Always a loving daughter to her parents and grandparents
and an affectionate and caring sister to her 13 siblings.
She was first and foremost a devoted wife to my foster father
And a tenderhearted and loving mother to me.
That was my Mom!

She never uttered a negative word about anyone.
She saw only the good in people, their strengths and talents
Overlooking their foibles and failings
and celebrating their talents, accomplishments, and successes.
Deeply religious but totally free of bigotry.
That was my Mom!

I'm sure that she knows, and with deepest regret,
that she missed the arrival of five of her six grandchildren,
12 great grandchildren, and two great great grandchildren.
How they would have loved her!
But they were deprived of those blessings.
It has now been several years since she left us,
but she has never been far from our thoughts and prayers,
She was one of a kind.
That was my Mom!

My Dad

His blood courses trough my veins.
An Irishman through and through
Steel-willed and hard-working
With talented hands and agile mind
Unable to show affection
But you knew that he loved you

My Mother-in-Law

Mothers-in-law usually get "bad press."
At best, they have been a "laugh line,"
the brunt of jokes—
at worst, vilified, and devalued,
belittled and ridiculed.
But not all of them deserve
reproach or disparagement.
I knew and loved one who,
although misunderstood by many,
was a wonderful woman, mother of
two sons and two daughters,
A World War II Gold Star Mother,
when Tommy was Killed in Action,
a Navy medic serving with the Marines
at Peliliu in the Pacific in 1944.
But she was also a wonderful grandmother
She was Lillian Maria Ingabor Ahola,
a Finnish-American woman
of many talents, including skilled stenciler,
superb plain comfort food kitchener
and creator of gourmet Finnish dishes,
gifted painter, and accomplished seamstress.

But Lillian possessed a formidable demeanor,

seemingly hard-nosed, cold, and unyielding.

To my children, when they were young,

she was Sergeant Bilco, tough and unbending,

hardheaded and unsentimental.

until they discovered her sensitivity,

her tender heart, her vulnerability, her unconditional love.

And they returned that love six-fold

to make her last years warm and happy, wondrous, and

rewarding.

Nanni's Legacy

When a wife, mother, teacher, and friend dies,
An important part of the world dies with her.
Whatever constituted her being
— her walk, tone of voice, opinions, appearance,
use of language, humor, sense of style and beauty,
personality. personal history, talents,
and even her smile—all disappear forever.
Everything dies, but the reverberations
of her impact on the lives of others
— her husband, her children and grandchildren,
her relatives, students, friends, and acquaintances,
linger on and endure forever.
So when Nanni died, she left a legacy
of grace, of beauty. of helpfulness, of caring,
and of unconditional love
to all who were fortunate enough to meet and know her.
She was a blessing forever to be missed
and never to be forgotten.

A Wonderful Week

It was the week of 23 July 2006
A shimmering summer of special days and nights
Embellished with good company and great repasts.
Four of my children and my closest friend and companion
With me or near me all of those days.
All told, a rare and much appreciated
Time of warmth, comfort, and happiness.

It was especially heart warming
To see my sons enjoying the company of their younger sister
And to observe her love for and devotion to her big brothers.
But, there was also the bonus of the complete
Acceptance and affection shown by the new love of my life,
For my sons and daughter
And the caring and tenderness returned to her by my progeny.

And then there was the fun of sharing of household chores,
— The laundry, bed changing, dishwashing —
— The cooking, serving, and cleanup of the sumptuous meals
— — Spaghetti and meat balls, roasted chicken with all the
fix'ins,
The baked stuffed pork chops, medium rare roast beef,
the chicken Parmesan,
The bacon or sausage and eggs, the French toast.

But, most of all there were the feelings
of harmony, affinity, and concord,
The pervasiveness of contentment, fulfillment, and love.
A very special time in our lives—one never to be forgotten.

To a Young Father

Today is a special day for you.
You were your parents' first child,
a son to protect, cherish, and love.
Now, the human cycle has continued
with the birth of your son.
You now have the weighty responsibility
of doing all those wonderful things
that good parents do —
guiding, teaching, and supporting
his upbringing, schooling, interests, and hobbies —
yes, even carefully and thoughtfully
correcting and disciplining
when such actions are necessary,
but always loving him unconditionally.
And, from my knowledge and personal observation,
you have discharged your obligations to your son
fully, unstintingly, admirably, and lovingly.
My hope for you is that he will appreciate
all that you are doing for him and will achieve
whatever he and you wish for his future.
He obviously has the intelligence and the talent
to do great things with his life
with your and his mother's encouragement and help.
So, my wish for you on your birthday,
from deep within my heart,
is for all good and happy things
such special days impart.
I wish you and those closest to you,
the ones you love the best — your saintly mom,
your handsome and talented son,
your brothers and sisters,
and whomever else you choose —
peace, hope, and love,
and health and happiness too.

For My Grandson

Life is fleeting, years rush past...
and little boys grow up so fast!
Let me take time to be
thankful my grandson's here with me.
And though I'm far away most days,
let me take time to play.
Let me take time to smile
to sit with him for just a while.
Let me take time for walks,
for swings and sports
and quiet talks,
for sharing tickles, laughs, and hugs
for patching knees
and catching bugs...
for running races, for climbing trees,
for helping with his ABCs...
for hatching plots
and planning schemes
for listening to his thoughts and dreams.
Let me tuck him in at night,
hear his prayers, turn off the light...
and when my busy day is done,
let me thank God for him.

On Your Wedding Day

Today is the second most important day of your lives.
The day of your birth was the first.
You don't even remember that wonderful and historic event.
However, you'll always remember this day — I guarantee it!
It marks the beginning of your new life,
a life you fully share for the first time
with any other being.

For today, you have given each other the greatest gift
that anyone can give to another —
total love and commitment, mind, body, and soul,
now and forevermore.
Our family, relatives, and friends rejoice with you
on this most auspicious of all days,
and wish for you on all days henceforth,
every blessing that God and his people can bestow.
Among them, long and productive lives,
fitness and vitality, joy and happiness,
and everything that will be useful to you in God's purpose.

And I have one other heartfelt wish for you.
My hope and prayer is that you have children,
loving, healthy, and happy children,
if that be God's plan and your wish,
because that, in my own experience,
is the greatest gift of all.

God love you both, this day and always.
Love and felicitations.

Steadfastness

Falling in love is easy
Staying in love is trying
But worth the effort

My Daughter-in-Law

A woman of bounteous and exceptional beauty and charm
Owner of a prodigious repertoire of skills that disarms.
Ever a graceful hostess, considerate and without compare
With a flair for the winning rejoinder "en cher."
A lady-like demeanor, with sweetness her weapon of choice
Along with an astute ability to mollify with grace.
That's my daughter-in-law!
Always plain-spoken, but never harsh or cynical
Blessed with an endearing Spanish accent
But with an amazingly expansive English vocabulary
Occasionally unyielding, but never intractable.
Always thoughtful but never patronizing
Typically unpredictable, but invariably dependable.
Unconventionally authentic, and relentlessly resolute
Always precise and exacting, but invariably accessible.
That's my daughter-in-law!
In name, looks, physiognomy, demeanor, and personality,
she is unique, a one-of-a-kind masterpiece of femininity.
She is first and foremost a devoted wife to my son,
truly a helpmate as well as a paramour,
and a tenderhearted mother to my grandchildren.
She is also an indulged daughter to her parents

And a loving sister to her siblings,

and an attentive and caring daughter-in-law

to her father-in-law."

That's my daughter-in-law!

But, to all who really know her,

she is more than a devoted wife,

mother, sister, and daughter.

she is a loyal and much-treasured friend to many.

One who is always supportive, concerned and caring,

a warm and effective champion,

a trusted confrere and confidant

and an affectionate and loving companion.

After God made her, He destroyed the mold.

That's my daughter-in-law!

Great Granddaughter on Her 2nd Birthday

Since the first time I saw you, and every time since then,

I have often noted that you were not even two.

Yet, you were so alert, so vivacious,

so bright, so strong-willed, so high spirited and feisty, too.

Still you were invariably good-natured,

genial and happy, affectionate, loving, and true.

So, my great granddaughter is a remarkable child,

A beautiful little girl to have and to hold.

I am blessed to have lived long enough to know her,

and hope that the Lord will give me many more years

to observe, love, and enjoy her.

For My Granddaughters

Why do I love you?

Because you are my granddaughter? Naturally!

Because you are talented and gifted? Oh, Yes!

Because you are intelligent and precocious? You bet!

Because you are pretty and enchanting? Indeed!

Because you are animated and cheerful? Of course!

Because you are warm and amiable? Absolutely!

Because you are kind and affectionate? Certainly!

Because you are dutiful and faithful? Assuredly!

Because you are caring and loving? By all means!

So, your grandfather loves you

because of those sterling qualities.

Gifts to him, your parents, siblings, aunts,

uncles, cousins, and friends.

Blessings that have made their and your

lives better and happier.

But, most of all, he loves you just because you're you,

A one-of-a-kind masterwork

of God, our Father, with the cooperation of your parents

and countless generations of ancestors

from Europe, the Middle East, Asia,

North and South America and Africa.

That's Who

Who has surprised and intimidated me
with an unexpected phone call —
and without identifying herself?
My daughter-in-law, that's who!

Who uses language that would make
an old salt like me blush and take cover?
My daughter-in-law, that's who!
Who always has time to spend
sharing stories and experiences
that seem ever new?
My daughter-in-law, that's who!

Who compliments my cooking
and backs it up with a prodigious appetite?
My daughter-in-law, that's who!
Who has a new grandchild named Grace
who's the apple of her eye?
My daughter-in-law, that's who!

Who loves her family, both immediate and extended,
and never fails to show it?
My daughter-in-law, that's who!
Who is one of my favorite daughters-in-law
(and that's a big secret never to be revealed)?
So now it's your turn — guess who!

Guess Who

This one is special
Because she is lovable
And sweetly naughty

Great Granddaughter on Her 1st Birthday

Today is your birthday —your First
It's an auspicious day for you, but it is special for me, too,
because it marks the anniversary
of the day when your Mom, my granddaughter,
brought into this world a beautiful daughter,
a wonderful gift to her Husband and her Mom and Dad,
and a marvelous gift to me —
my very first great grandchild.

Over one year ago, God began a good work in you,
and will complete that work in the many years to come.
My prayers for you now are these:
That your love for your
parents, grandparents, many great-aunts and uncles,
and many cousins
will increase in depth and strength
as the days and years go by.
That you will have a long, healthy, and happy life.
That you will continue to grow abundantly
in knowledge, skills, and insights of every kind.
That will you learn by vital experience
what really matters in life?

That on that day many months and years from now
when you appear before God,
He welcomes you as a flawless gift,
your having earned a rich harvest of praise
for a long, productive, and virtuous life.
Offered with great love
through our Lord, Jesus Christ, Amen.

Granddaughter On Her 8th Birthday

Another year has passed

And your talents and beauty continue unsurpassed.

Added to those sterling qualities are

Your bright mind and sweet disposition.

You're a blessing to all who appreciate a first-class lass —

Especially your Poppi who admires and loves you

For all of the days, hours, and minutes that have passed.

So, here is a special prayer and a wish for you:

May you always see God's Light on the path ahead

May troubles never turn your heart to stone.

And may you always remember

When shadows fall you do not walk alone.

And realize, too, that God and your family love you,

love that will always be true no matter what you do.

And may the friendships you make be ones that endure,

and that any gray clouds be small ones for sure.

And trusting in Him to whom we all pray,

may a song fill your heart, every step of the way.

For Maura

All the dreams I prayed you'd be,
are all they things you are.
You were once my little girl,
and now you're my shining star.

The fair-skinned little girl
with the blonde ponytail,
The little doll that I called "Peanut"
because she was so petite.
She was our "little mother,"
taking care of her baby brother,
carting him around the house on her hip.
He called her "Maw Maw."

My little girl grew healthy and strong,
and showed what she could do
by managing and establishing
several Gloria Stevens figure salons.
Now she has a daughter of her own,
a lovely and talented young lady.
So Maura, Laine, and husband Sam
live happily together in Rome.

She means a lot to me
because she is so bright and caring.
And I'm so proud of her
— a take-charge woman
with a heart of gold.

Peanut

She is wondrous
Because she has a big heart
And cares totally

For Kathy

The little girl with the big brown eyes
and the ponytail
that I called Pidge, short for Pigeon.

The little girl who told me
that when sitting on my lap
and I sang or talked to her,
her ears "buzzed."

The little girl I took to school
on her first day at Spaulding
and who reluctantly let go of my hand
and bravely said goodbye
through her tears,
causing me to leave quickly before she saw
the tears rolling down my cheeks.

The little girl who once told me,
"I love you, Daddy.
When I grow up I'm going to marry you."
And now she is the "big girl"
one who looks so much like her mother
and who shares her mother's
helpfulness to others, her love of children,
and her skills as a teacher.

All the dreams I prayed you'd be,
Are all they things you are.
You were once my little girl,
And now you're my shining star.

A 60th Birthday Assessment

Precocious from birth and thriving thereafter!
The only one of my four sons who followed me around
when I was building or repairing something —
he was my work buddy, a relationship that I treasured.
Blessed with innumerable and formidable talents
and an insatiable appetite for answers to such questions as
What makes it work? Why does it do that?
How can we fix it? When can I try it?
He soon became more expert than his teacher.

Preferring large houses and sturdy vehicles, tools,
appliances, devices, apparel, and accouterments.
He learned to be a haggler par excellence — numero uno!
An expert sailor and navigator,
with a love of sailing and a healthy respect for the sea.
An accomplished swimmer and skier,
punctuated by Senior Life Saver
and Water Safety and First Aid certifications.
An avid and truly accomplished fisherman
whether for fresh water fly-casting, lake angling, surf casting, or
deep sea trolling — for trout, bass, stripers, cod, or game fish.

An ardent and respectable golfer but above all a competitor.
An accomplished musician in earlier years
notably prodigious in terms of vocals and musicianship on the
baritone sax and brilliance in comedic performance.
Never profane or blasphemous.
Under no circumstances irreverent or impious.
Typically predictable and invariably dependable.
Relentlessly thoughtful and unfailingly authentic,
Prudent and serious, but accessible and open.
An aficionado of food and drink, an accomplished cook
whether using a grill, an oven, a deep oil cooker, or a stove top

He is a bona fide chef and passionate gourmand
and shows a propensity for frequenting expensive restaurants
and drinking top-of-the-top-shelf beverages.
invariably with unusual capacity, absolutely no signs of
overindulgence, and with undeniable and total aplomb!

In other domains, he is a genuinely creative and gifted genius
And again with a prodigious repertoires of skills.
He is a master builder and fixer-upper,
whether the task involves electronics, plumbing, masonry,
carpentry, acoustics, lighting, photography, directing,
video production, or videoediting

You name it, and he can do it — and do it well.
Here is the other side of Bill, the family man:
A man for whom his Mom, Dad, and Siblings
have always been proud.
A caring and devoted husband
And a doting father to his children;
His family means everything to him.
But, to all who really know, respect, and love him
He is more than a determined and faithful family man
And a talented and successful businessman.
He is a much-loved son, husband, father,
brother, uncle, and friend —
one who is always supportive and helpful,
To all with whom he comes in contact.
After God made him, He shredded the blueprint.
That's Bill Jr.

My Eldest

A serious guy
who cares what is happening
to those he loves much

My Grandson

Who is nine years old today —and acts 15?
Who speaks English and Spanish fluently
and with an amazingly large vocabulary?
Who's bright and amiable, fun-loving, and talented?
Who visits me on the Cape when he can
and keeps me intrigued — and amused?
Who never fails to thank me for my poems and gifts
(a lost courtesy for most young people)?

Throughout my life I've received many gifts that I hold dear.
Those gifts include those who loved me and are no longer here
your Nanni, Kathleen, and my three sisters and three brothers,
But, the greatest gift I have received in all my days
is the one great gift made up of separate parts,
each one an individual gift
and each one securely resting in my heart.

This is the gift that made my life complete,
and at every thought of it my heart skips a beat.
This gift is one that God sent to me
—one that is perfect and uniquely mine.
It is my family: my six children (your aunts and uncles),
twelve grandchildren (your first cousins),
and the pair of great grandchildren (your first cousins
once and twice removed) that God has given to me.

But, for whatever the reason,
and known only to God and not to me,
there is one element of that marvelous gift of family
that has been very special to me.
That's my Grandson, you see!

For My Grandson on His 18ᵗʰ Birthday

Another birthday has arrived,
And it is an auspicious one,
Next in importance to your 21ˢᵗ.
For today your can do some things
That according to many,
And in many states,
You could not do yesterday.
They'll go unidentified here

Because one of the new choices
Now available to you
Is one that I hope and pray you'll
Choose to avoid.
I think you know what it is anyway.

That being said,
I wish for you today and every day
And every night I specifically pray:
That you will enjoy a long,
Healthy, happy, and productive life,

That you will find a true vocation —
A line of work that you really love —
That you will prepare yourself carefully
And completely for that profession,
Occupation, business, trade,
Craft, art, or calling.
And that you will enjoy success in that lifework.

A Life Lesson

Golf is demanding
It challenges one's mettle
And rewards patience

Twin Sons on Their 58th Birthday

Your Mom and I first learned of your impending arrival
on or about October 18, 1948;
that is, about one week before your were born.
To say that Dr. Simmons' revelation was a surprise
is a gross understatement.
It was a bolt from the blue that kept on shocking!

Little did we know how much your birth would change our
lives!
Bill Jr. was less than 16 months old, still in diapers,
and not sleeping through the night.
Then he was joined by two colicky, geyser-spewing,
up-chucking little male bundles of joy —
which kept one or both of their parents up every night—
changing their diapers and crib bedding
and attempting to stop their crying by rocking them to sleep.

It was an interesting time — a period of several months —
that resulted in a stomach ulcer for me
and an understandable case of "run-a-way wife."
She took a trolley to Fitchburg
and a train to Charlestown, New Hampshire
to her Aunt Margareeta's for comfort and TLC;
she had experienced about all she could stand for
from her progeny and me.
I chased her there the next day
and begged her to come back home with me.
She agreed after intense persuasion and many promises.
Inevitably, things improved— the up-chucking stopped,
and the three of the cutest baby boys anyone had ever seen
smiled, laughed, and cooed — and slept through the night!
The Tracey family was the talk (all complimentary)
of the town of Ashby — and later, of Townsend!

For the most part, life was great for everyone.
Although we were not wealthy (many people thought we were),
we lived well and, over the next few years,
we were joined by Kathy and Maura and, still later, by Sean.

All three of the older boys served Mass together at St. John's,
Then the dance band, marching band, and town band gigs started,
and the fame of the Tracey family grew and spread
until the Tracey boys' band morphed into The Prodigy,
the crowd-pleasing and much acclaimed nightclub show band.

Although there were a few bumps in the road —
Brian's fall at the VFW pond
and his problems with the teacher at North Middlesex High School
(resulting in his transfer to the Brothers High School in Fitchburg
and subsequent success in school and college).
the years at Linden Acres in Townsend were memorable.
So many wonderful and rewarding memories flood my mind —
recollections that I treasure
because they validate my belief that, as a family,
we had something very special.
It was the product of your Mom's guidance (if not insistence),
wishes, and prayers.

I am so proud of my children, their accomplishments,
their togetherness, and love for each other regardless
(or perhaps because of) their differences
in interests, preferences, and personalities.

I hope and pray that the closeness will remain
with all of our children for the rest of their lives.
It is so unusual in this day and age —
and so irreplaceable — a real blessing from God.
I'm confident that their devotion to each other,

remarked about and admired by so many,
will endure and strengthen.

I am especially proud of and deeply grateful
for the creativity, entrepreneurship,
perseverance, perspicacity, perceptiveness,
talents, and love of all of my sons.
Those traits are also gifts from Our Maker.
to their father as well as to each other.

So, on this auspicious day,
I say thank you, Kevin and Brian, and God,
for being what you are and mean to me and to each other.
— HAPPY BIRTHDAY

Great Granddaughter #2 on Her 1st Birthday

When your Great Grandfather was a young man,
He had two bonny daughters,
One of them was your Great Aunt Maura
And your Great Aunt Kathy was the other.
At bedtime before they went to sleep,
I often sang songs to them
To help them reach the Land of Oz
With happy thoughts to keep.

One ditty was *Too-ra Loo-ra Loo-ra*, a lovely Irish lullaby.
Although I will never "croon" it for you in person
Know that I sing it now from miles away—
an offering of much love, one that is past due
But I'm sure your Daddy when you ask him,
will sing it just for you."

My Grandson on His 29th Birthday

According to your peers, you're approaching an important milestone
your thirtieth birthday, the age of full maturity —
but, again, according to your confreres,
it marks the beginning of an unavoidable downhill slide
in your physical and mental capacities.
That's nonsense — claptrap, hogwash, and bunk
— out-and-out B.S.
Don't believe it, even for a moment.

The fact of the matter is that your very best years lie ahead.
So, now is the time to plan to make the most of them.
while you're still in your twenties —
a great decade to be in,
even if it's the last year in that eventful era.

You have been successful already!
You started a business and have survived for six years
when most new companies fail within two years.
That's a major accomplishment, one that you should be proud of,
and one that makes me very proud of my grandson!

Let me remind you again that you have someone Above,
your Nanni who loved you so very much in life
and will always watch over you from Heaven—
someone who only wants the very best of everything
that love, prayers, and life can offer you.

My wish too for your birthday is for all the good and special
things such notable days impart. I wish you
and the ones you love the best — your Mom and Dad, Sister,
Niece, and Goddaughter, and whomever else you choose —
good health, prosperity, and happiness,
and most of all, peace, hope, and love, too.

Granddaughter on Her 20ᵗʰ Birthday

A young woman with many accomplishments
Always and everywhere second to none,
And with an abundance of plaudits yet to come.
Having a 2ⁿᵈ Degree Black Belt in Karate certification
and membership in the Zen Do Kai Martial Arts Association,
She is fully capable of taking care of herself in a confrontation.

A 2007 graduate of Manhattan's Berkeley
higher education institution,
with a Bachelor of Science degree securely in hand.
Having chosen Marketing as her field of concentration
earned with a 4.000 Grade Point Average,
a standard seldom achieved and worthy of acclamation.
Finding elite employment with the Chase Manhattan
corporation
holding investment banking large in her expectations.

Titled by Chase as a Personal Banker
and working toward the impressive credential
of Chartered Financial Consultant
a financial planning designation. Aha!
awarded only by the American College of Bryn Mawr.
A member of the International Honor Society at Berkeley
she successfully completed the NASD Series 6 Investment
Company Variable Annuity Mutual Fund Sales Examination
and scheduled to sit for the NASS Sixty-Three.

But allow me to put aside those achievements for the moment
to include a special 23ʳᵈ birthday admonishment —
as well as a special wish just for you —
one that I hope will help make your dreams come true.
With age comes more and more responsibility
and adulthood inevitably results in large doses of reality.

Always remember that God and your family love you,
something that will always be true no matter what you do.
Although circumstances in your life are bound to change,
know that God's and you family's love remain.

So, if some of your days aren't what you want them to be,
there will be more days that will be rewarding, you'll see!
So, live every day as if it were you last,
and never repeat the mistakes of your past.

May the friendships you make be those which endure,
And all your gray clouds be small ones for sure.
And trusting in Him to whom all we pray,
may a song fill your heart, every step of the way.

About My Dad and Me

I loved my dad.
Despite the anguish of the past
When we were separated first by miles,
Which he tried to overcome by long-distance travel to me
And then by restrictions imposed by his second wife
Who mothered four of my siblings and two half-brothers
And felt unable to add me to her burden.
Understandable to me now, but not at age six.
So, I remained with my foster parents
Through grade school, high school, and college.
When I returned from serving in World War II
And got to know and love my dad
For the few short years that remained of his life
Unfortunately he never got to meet
Five of his six grandchildren
— and they never experienced the love of their grandfather.
What an unfortunate state of affairs!

For My 4th Daughter-in-Law on Her Birthday

If I said to you in person the words that follow,
We'd probably both be embarrassed.
But, when the words go unspoken,
As they almost always do,
The words of respect and love
are always in my heart.

Yet, I still want you to know
How much I appreciate and value
Your being the extraordinary mother
Of my beautiful grandchildren.
The wife of my son,
And (if I may say so) my very special friend.

That's why I'm celebrating you —
A warm and gifted woman
Who has enriched our family
With her sterling qualities and prodigious talents
And given so much to all who know and love her.

What better time than today,
And in this way,
To tell you how much you're admired and loved?
So, that's why you're wished a day
As special as you are.
May your special day be full,
Your life be long
And your days as sweet
As an Irish song.
HAPPY BIRTHDAY!

For My Daughter's Birthday

Every time we're together
(which is not often enough for me,
although I know that time, distance,
and sometimes illness get in the way),
I discover something else that delights me
about my Daughter.

In name, looks, demeanor, and personality,
as well as her talents
as a teacher, wife, mother, and grandmother,
she is the mirror image of her Mother,
That's Pigeon, my Kathy!

I recall so very often of the special times
we enjoyed together — especially in Townsend
when she tiptoed down stairs
to sit on my lap and talk
when everyone else was asleep upstairs.

And every time we're apart,
I think about her and pray every night
that she is ok — happy and pain free.

So, let me close with a special prayer:
Heavenly Father, I thank you for your gifts to me.
On this day and in a grateful way,
I thank you sincerely for my daughter,
my Pigeon, my Kathy
who is very special to her Daddy.

Twin Sons' 58th Birthday Assessment

Identical twins with matching DNA
Indistinguishable at birth,
but recognizably distinctive in adulthood,
but growing more alike as they approach retirement age.
Both men have abundant and formidable talents.
And insatiable appetites for expensive hobbies—
airplanes (twin engine), sailboats (large ones),
cars (Cadillacs) and motorcycles (Harley Davidsons)
That's Kevin and Brian
They are expert sailors and navigators,
with a love of sailing and a healthy respect for the sea.
Accomplished swimmers and skiers,
punctuated by Senior Life Saver's
and Water Safety and First Aid Instructor certification
Notably prodigious musicianship
and brilliance in performance —
whether on piano, organ, trumpet, trombone,
French horn, violin, banjo, bass guitar, bongos, or voice —
underscored by their ability to "work a room,"
individually or in tandem.
That's Kevin and Brian
Occasionally profane, but never blasphemous.
Often irreverent, but never impious.
Sometimes unpredictable, but invariably dependable.
Roguishly authentic, but relentlessly upbeat.
Affable and garrulous, accessible and open.
Avid golfers, but with suspiciously low handicaps.
Aficionados of food and drink, bona fide gourmands.
but with a propensity to frequent expensive restaurants
and drink top-of-the-top-shelf beverages. (with aplomb!)
That's Kevin and Brian

In other domains, they are truly creative and gifted geniuses,
but of somewhat dissimilar,
yes, even distinctively different genre
And again with a prodigious
but sometimes disparate repertoires of skills.

One is an accomplished and persuasive public speaker,
An astute and sagacious marketer,
and a brilliant branding evangelist. That's Kevin.

The other is an accomplished vocalist
and prodigious instrumentalist
A charming and disarming performer
With a visage and persona that the camera,
whether still or TV, loves.
That's Brian.
A caring and devoted husband to Janice
And a doting and adoring father to Kolby and Kaylyn
That's Kevin.

An attentive and loving husband to Joanne
And a tenderhearted and cherishing father to Jackie and Mikie
That's Brian

But, to all who really know them
They are more than talented, lovable, bon vivante, debonair,
and successful people and businessmen.
They are loyal and much-loved sons, husbands, fathers,
brothers, uncles, and friends —
Ones who are always supportive and helpful,
Warm and effective advocates, and generous benefactors.
After God made Kevin and Brian, He destroyed the mold.

My Grandson on His 19ᵗʰ Birthday

So, another birthday has arrived!

It marks the beginning of the end of your teen years.

I sincerely hope that it also brings some good events

during some of the best years of your young life

In the meantime, here is a birthday prayer for you:

I pray that on this special day,

God will touch your heart in a beautiful way.

I pray that His power from Heaven above

will bless your life and fill it with love.

I pray that He grants you special care

so that you'll know that He's always there.

I pray too that you feel His love for you

in all you ever say, think, believe, or do.

For someone as special as you,

now facing some decisions about your future,

along with your Mom and Dad, I'm sure

we're hoping God grants you good health and much elation.

I know He'll do that sooner than "then,"

so for your Happy Birthday I ask this today, Amen.

Elder Daughter on Her Birthday

A woman of abundant and exceptional charm
Owner of a prodigious repertoire of skills that disarms.
Ever a charming hostess, debonair and without compare
With a flair for the gracious rejoinder "en cher."
A lady-like demeanor, with sweetness her weapon of choice
Along with an astute ability to disarm with grace.
That's Pigeon, my Kathy

Always plain-spoken, but never irreverent
Occasionally unyielding, but never obstinate.
Always thoughtful but never overbearing.
Typically predictable, but invariably dependable.
Conventionally authentic, and relentlessly steadfast.
Always precise and exacting, but invariably open.
That's Pigeon, my Kathy.

But, to all who really know her,
She is more than a devoted wife, mother,
Grandmother, sister, and daughter
And a gifted and caring teacher,
She is a loyal and much-treasured friend to many
One who is always supportive,
A warm and effective advocate,
And an affectionate and loving woman

After God made her, He destroyed the mold.
That's Pigeon, my Kathy!

My Pigeon

Hearing her is great.
Being with her is better.
Then I am happy

On the 10th Anniversary of My Wife's Death

You know, and I'm sure with deepest regret,
that you were not here to welcome
and love your four newest grandchildren,
and your two great grandchildren.
How they would have loved you!
But they were deprived of those blessings.

It has now been ten years since you left us,
but you have never been far from our thoughts and prayers.
and for me, the wonderful memories of the 56 magical years
we shared and enjoyed together.
Those years were filled with joy and love
As well a few challenges and heartaches.

You were a lovely and remarkable woman.
You never uttered a negative word about anyone.
As usual, you saw only the good in people
and their strengths.
Your belief in and support made it possible for me
to accomplish what I didn't believe was achievable.

As for our children and grandchildren,
you overlooked their foibles and failings
and celebrated their talents,
successes, and accomplishments.
Meeting you was the best thing
that ever happened to me.
Marrying you rewarded me
with the best years of my life.
I thank God every day
for bringing you to me,
the most priceless gift of my life.

Love

When you love a lot
You love with all of your heart
That's the way it is!

The Meaning of Love

Love is a wish —
for the best that life offers
for a son or daughter.

Love is a prayer —
for good health and happiness
for a relative or friend.

Love is a gift —
for the giver as well as for
the one who receives it.

Love is faith —
in the goodness, the worthiness
of another person, even a stranger.

Love is companionship —
the togetherness that makes life worthwhile

Love is an emotion —
strong and overpowering
but also so hard to find and keep.

My Very First Love

It was the early spring of forty-one,
I was an eight-to-five working man,
a shirt-shop shortage chaser,
at the Cluett and Peabody Arrow Shirt factory.
She was a high school student,
at age 17, about one year younger than I.

We met at Dolly McDaid's School of Dancing,
on upper North Street, beyond Rindge Road,
where we met weekly on Friday nights, eight to ten
for two hours of dancing and funtastics
(she was a wonderfully skillful dancer),
followed by an hour or two
of parking and spooning in my Pop's 1936 Pontiac.

We soon became an "item," "going steady," as they said.
We were "in love!"
Our weekly dates became more frequent
as we began to enjoy dancing the foxtrot,
waltz, cha cha cha, rumba, polka, and jitterbug together,
played by the big bands at the Totem Pole
Canobie Lake, Kimball's Starlight, and Whalom Park ballrooms.

We danced to the music of Glenn Miller, Artie Shaw,
Gene Krupa, Fats Waller, Lawrence Welk, Vaughn Monroe,
Tommy Dorsey, Duke Ellington, Harry James, Kaye Kaiser,
Benny Goodman, Charlie Barnett, and Glenn Gray,
We slow-danced and danced "close" to Moonglow, Dream,
Two Sleepy People, It's Only a Paper Moon, Amapola, Dolores,
Tangerine, I Had the Craziest Dream, Blueberry Hill, Paper Doll,
Night and Day, and Star Dust.

And we jitterbugged to I've Got a Gal in Kalamazoo,
Woodchoppers' Ball, Jumpin' At the Woodside, Caravan,
One O'clock Jump, Bugle Boy of Company B,
Stompin' At the Savoy, and In the Mood.

By the end of the year,
I was seeing her at her home on Myrtle Avenue,
meeting her mother, and her father,
who worked at Simond's Saw & Steel),
being a frequent guest for dinner, and sharing the "Privacy"
of the front stairs with her sister, Doris and her friend, Freddie.
conversing but mostly hugging and kissing.

In the fall of forty-one I entered college as a freshman
and became deeply involved in all the activities of the college
—collegiate soccer and basketball, parties and dances,
Glee Club, Drama Club, Winter Carnival preparations,
was elected class president, and met the girl
who was to become my wife, Kathleen.

One of our last dates was just before Christmas 1941,
I gave "my love" a gold ring with a small stone
(I believe it was blue),
not an engagement ring, but a friendship ring.
It was the last time I saw her until years later,
at the Worcester Auditorium after World War II,
when we were married,
I to Kathleen, and "my love" to Eddie,
and we danced together again without missing a step.

Crooner or Chanteuse

A song is a gift
To the singer and audience
A blessing from God

The Risk of Loving

Love for another is a very intriguing emotion.

It comes unbidden, like a thief in the night.

So, it is never something planned,

not even something earned.

It happens without thought or effort.

It is given without thought of compensation.

And when love happens, it cannot be rejected,

turned off because it may be risky

or even painful.

I have experienced that enigma

because I loved someone,

a woman, a young woman,

with my whole heart, soul, strength, and mind,

a woman that I couldn't have because she loved

and was committed to someone else.

I did not seek her out,

nor did I choose to love her,

I'm convinced that it was God's work

because I needed someone so much.

My children sympathized with me.

They told me that the risk

to my emotional health was formidable.

they couldn't understand that I am already hurt,

that I had already suffered the damage,

and that I could not regain my emotional balance

unless that woman was a part of my life.

I loved her without reservation.

And believed that I would continue to love her

for what remained of my time,

bitter sweet though the relationship might be.

I needed her in my life

regardless of the heartache, the anguish

that were certain to result.

Post note: My children were

right!

The risk of permanent danger

to my psyche was great.

I was fortunate to survive

that episode of my life.

I now have completely

recovered!

The Power of My Love

My love is strong enough to meet
the most challenging things....
the crushing waves that overwhelm
the soul,
the howling winds that leave
one dazed and breathless,
the sudden storms beyond
my life's control.
My love is also strong enough to meet
the everyday stuff....
the commonplace, the mundane
the ordinary, run-of-the-mill things —
the jibes, the sharp retorts,
even the lack of sensitivity of others.

My love is also strong enough to meet
the smallest things...
the trivial troubles
that persist and annoy —
the insect-size travails, buzzing
and unrelenting,
the shrieking wheels that rasp and grate
upon my joy.

From My Wife

I have love you too much to ever forget
the love you have spoken to me
and the kiss of affection still warm on my lips
when you told me how true you would be.
I know not if fortune be fickle or friend
or if time on your memory wears.

I know that I love you wherever you roam,
and remember you live in my prayers.
Go where you will on land or sea,
I'll share all your sorrows and cares.
And, at night when I kneel by my bedside to pray,
I'll remember you, love, in my prayers.

When You Love Someone

When you love someone

So much for so long,

And you lose her,

You have so much love unexpended,

That you have to love again

Before it smothers you.

That's what happened to me.

When I lost my wife.

I had so much unused love

That it was choking me.

And then I met someone.

So lovely, so warm, so caring.

She released the floodgates

of my love,

and it embraced her.

I was healed!

First Love

She wasn't my first girl.
Before I met her,
there were many other girls in my life —
Some of the most memorable were
Theresa, Jane, Mary, Jean, Janet, and Lucille —
one Italian, two Polish, two French Canadian, and
one Irish— and all of them young, comely,
interesting, and warm.

But, I knew before many dates had passed,
with the exception of one of almost a year's courtship,
that none was the girl of my dreams.
I finally met her in September 1941,
the first month of my freshman year in college.

She was an elfin-like creature not quite five feet tall,
weighing less than one hundred pounds.
and with long wavy dark brown hair.
dark and luminous brown eyes. and peaches-and-cream skin,
a lilting voice, a warm personality, and Irish-Finnish lineage,

She wore a plaid skirt, a lavender blouse,
silk hose with the seams up the back,

and brown and white saddle shoes.
With a smile that would light up a room,
a soft and melodious voice,
and an easy and a sweet-sounding laugh,
I was smitten at first sight
and immediately asked her for a date.
To my surprise, she agreed,
and that very night we drove to a chain restaurant.
I don't remember what we ordered,
but I do remember that I was too nervous to eat!

Within minutes, I knew that she was the girl
I had been searching for, the one for me.
Before I dropped her off at her house,
I told her that some day I would marry her.
And I did, the day before I left for the Pacific War.

More than sixty years have passed
since that memorable night.
many years of happiness,
tempered by a few months of challenge and sadness
scattered among those
rewarding and scintillating spans of time.
But, all in all it added up to a wonderful life.

On Finding Each Other

Our bond continues to astound me.
Things feel so relaxed and comfortable between us
that it's like we've known each other forever.

Every time we're together
I discover something new
that charms and enchants me anew.
And when we're apart
I'm usually thinking about the next time
we'll be together.

I can't help myself for feeling
that we connect in some magical way.
We have so much pleasure and fulfillment
that one could say we were predestined
to find each other

Although I can't be certain that's true,
I do know that I'm incredibly glad
That we have each other now
and that we can begin anew.

Somebody Special

That's my girl,
a very special lady,
with a foxy and winning smile,
a warm and lively persona,
and a delightful repertoire of wiles.

She softens and balms my life,
comforts and lifts my spirit,
and with her incredible
youthfulness and vigor,
makes me young at heart.

She claims to be a good cook,
and that I can believe,
but the proof of the pudding
is when she delivers
— sauerkraut and pork
with Chardonnay wine,
for me and my special lady,
—whom I hope is all mine.

My Prayers

I continue to say my daily prayers
for me, someone special, and those she loves.
But my inner life feels arid and dreary.

I can find no peace, where in earlier years,
my spiritual practices nourished me.
I am now unhappy, desolate, and confused.
Knowing that true prayer is being with God.

I come from the Roman Catholic tradition,
a custom that petitions God and the Saints
for healing, protection, and wisdom.
I long to be able to express my gratitude
to God for bringing my special friend closer to me
and helping her honor my need to see her more often.

But I seem to say, write, or do things
that keep her at arms-length from me.
I must open my heart to the Divine Grace,
and maybe I'll have the warm and caring
relationship with her that I yearn.

The Unachievable Fantasy

It makes absolutely no sense,
and therein lies the beauty and wonder of it.
What is this event of radiance and marvel?
It's my love for a very young woman,
one who has committed herself to another,
an emotional setting that is so hopeless.

For the second time in my life,
the two events separated by sixty years,
I am wholly and incurably in love.
The difference is that this time
that love cannot be returned,
so I am anguished, desolated, heartbroken.

Unintentionally, I hurt her. So, what do I do now?
How can I regain the love I valued so much?
How can I deal with has happened to me
in the winter of my life?
I am disillusioned, discouraged, and depressed.
Once again I am grieving and deeply wounded,
something I never believed could happen, did happen.

On Valentine's Day

What can I say to you that you haven't heard before?
But, is it important that you hear something new,
some words that hopefully will soar and not bore?
I think it is pressing on such an auspicious day,
the day set aside for one to say
the thoughts not expressed often enough
throughout the year on other days

I think you know fully well how difficult
it is for me to bare my emotions.
You have known that truth
long before we became close friends.
It happens to be one of the failures
I have never been able to cast off.

So, let me try to tell you how much you mean to me,
how your companionship, affection, and caring,
have enriched my life so abundantly.
When we are together, whether having dinner,
home-cooked or restaurant-served,
attending a family function, watching TV,
or sharing the happenings of the day
I am comfortable and contented,
calm and serene, cheerful and carefree.

And that is the effect you always produce
on the real person that is truly me.
So, on this Special Day, even if we are apart.
I thank you for being you.
You will always be in my heart.

Open Your Heart

Close your eyes and open your heart.
It's not that difficult to do
And it's the right thing for you
If you'll just make the start.

Love me tomorrow
as you love me today
For without your love
I can only know sorrow.

So, close your eyes and open your heart
Find solace in the knowledge
That this will be the beginning
Of years of blissful existence.

Indulge me by accepting me,
as your soul mate
One who is desperately seeking
Your lifetime commitment.
Close your eyes and open your heart.

Heart's Desire

Become a lover
Search and find your true soul mate
And earn happiness

Times of Fulfillment

When I'm in your presence,
all my wants and needs cease.
From the loneliness of long weeks,
comes contentment, comes release.
Gone are the daily disappointments
and the events that brought me pain.
When I'm with you I find comfort,
strength to persevere when hope seems vain.
You seem to be sensitive of my every struggle,
from my self-doubts, you set me free.
The time I spend with you becomes more precious,
which I would like to spend on bended knee
I owe you so very much for your caring
and hope that it will last
the rest of my life.

I Love You

I love you, precious lady.
I love you so today.
My time with you is magical,
So help me find the way
To be with you more often
And to use that time well.
I love you dear lady
Hold me gently in your hand
For I need you beside me.
Come and help me understand
What I must do to keep you with me.
I need your respect and affection
To meet each day's new challenge,
I must win your heart.
For I depend on your for all my want
For the very air I breathe.

A Message for My Love

I am so happy and relieved
feeling that I have been reprieved.
To be back in your good graces,
the status I always needed

It was very disconcerting
to say something that was subject
to misinterpretation,
especially when my motivation
was simply to ensure your protection.

Now that the confusion is over,
we can get on with our lives —
friends now and forever,
and always without strife.

Although we are both hurting
for our lost spouses,
and the companionship we crave,
we now have each other —
we are both so needy for love.

Absolution

When you forsake me
I'm depressed and unhappy.
My healing: mercy!

My Daily Valentine

I truly am a fortunate man.
I have been blessed with many things
but only a few with strong emotional strings.
The very short list includes love
the most important gift received from Above.

Far greater than anything I have ever dreamed of,
It has been the largess of two loves
serially and sequentially, not just one,
an unusual bequest to any woman's son
The first was granted early in my life,
ever-new from Spring, through Summer and Fall
to the Winter of my life, the apex of it all
KLD, my love from youth to old age,
the other, EMB, the love in
the Winter of my life.

A precious gift when I needed someone,
one I didn't knowingly search for
but one whom I found by happy chance.
The harvest has been almost five years
of contentment, fulfillment, and happiness.
For those precious gifts, I thank EMB.

My Mood Today

The whispering winds speak softly
Through the early morning haze.
As my old mind seeks younger thoughts
And the long-gone vigor of more active days.

Yet my love for you
Burns strongly and brightly still.
Engulfing all the aches and pains that bedevil me
And gives me the courage to replace those infirmities
With the vitality and toughness
That were once my hallmark, my cachet.

So, for those strengths forever gone,
I substitute gentleness, devotion, and faithfulness
To me our friendship and love is a song
That soothes my body and soul.
And your companionship is a blessing
That makes my life whole.
Thank you, EMB,
For another year of happiness.

Daring or Foolhardy?

Loving is risky
But it also yields rewards
The greatest — returned love

In Gratitude

How can any man get lucky enough
To find a lovely woman who loves him?
Even at his age
And for what he is, flaws and all?

How can any man show his gratitude,
His heart-felt thanks,
For the affection and devotion
Of a lovely woman who cares for him,
Pancreatitis, high cholesterol,
Hypertension, shingles,
Atrial fibrillation with Coumadin prescription,
Beginning pattern baldness,
Age spots and all?

How can a man repay
those precious gifts
of warmth and affection,
do justice to that love and caring?
I don't know. I wish that I did,
But I don't have a clue.
However I shall continue to try
to demonstrate how much she means to me.

And I will remember always
that she gave me hope when I had none,
Friendship when I had lost one
Courage when I was down,
And time when I needed some;
That she gave me joy when I was hurting,
And love, when I needed it badly.
She is my priceless gift from above.

That's Who?

Who stays with me whenever she can
and always gives me a warm hug
when she comes in?
That's my EMB

Six years have passed so quickly!
Who is the one who has been
in my thoughts and prayers
during those magical years?
That's my EMB!

Who means so much to me —
The one whose companionship,
affection, and caring
have enriched my life so abundantly?
That's my EMB!

Who is in my thoughts and prayers
every day and every night
before I go to sleep
and arise in the morning?
That's my EMB!

Throughout my life I've received
many gifts that I hold dear,
but the greatest gift I have received
in the last ten years
is the great gift of companionship
from a lovely woman —
one whose image, ardor, and warmth
rest securely in my heart.
That's my EMB!

For My Paramour

I need to hold you close

Where you will remain forever

You can be sure

That things can only get better.

Through days and nights

I don't worry because

Everything is going to be all right.

No one, not a single person,

Can know and understand what I'm feeling.

Your recent hospitalization and travails

have left me reeling.

But your upbeat attitude and indomitable spirit

have inspired my admiration

and renewed my appreciation

of the remarkable and irresistible woman

for whom I have clearly developed an addiction —

an obsession that encompasses attraction, attention,

adulation, adoration, compulsion,

elation, consummation, and celebration.

So, here's to a extraordinary person.

an astonishing woman in every respect,

on this sixth anniversary of our commemoration

of Saint Valentine's Day.

Let me begin with this Irish proverb:

May you be blessed always with

a sunbeam to warm you

a moonbeam to charm you

a sheltering angel

so nothing can harm you.

And now allow me to tell you again

how much you mean to me —

and let me say it the Gaelic way:

If companionship means gladness,

and love begets joy,

then how can I start

to count all the smiles

you've brought to my heart?

My Girl

Her name is a melody.
Her voice is music to my ears.
Her beauty is a feast for my eyes
Her fragrance is a holiday for my senses
Her figure is a banquet for my glances
Her persona is solace for my depression.
Her warmth is comfort for my emptiness
Her affection is balm for my soul.
Her presence is a holiday for my psyche.
She is my gift from God.

My Friend and Companion

She is a part of my every day
and involved in every good deed.
She's all I think and dream about;
she's all that I need.
When she's away from me,
I'm not at peace.
But when she arrives, all my worries cease.
To hold her hand, to have her close
must have her near or my anxiety grows.
So I beg her, "Please don't ever go."
Because my days are brighter
when she is near,
And I feel so alone when she's not here.
Usually an old curmudgeon,
she makes me laugh and smile.
She never fails to make me feel worthwhile.
At the brink of reaching the age of eighty-five
I am grateful to the Lord for being alive.
I thank Him for my well-being and active mind
Which are worth more than the wealth that is not mine.
But I thank Him most fervently for the gift of EMB
She is, for me,
a one-of-a-kind and heaven-send gratuity.

My Love for You

My love for you grows with every heartbeat,
My time with you always feels so complete.
From the day we met again, I knew
The love we now share was real and true.

The times we're together are always so great
Just as it was that rainy summer night on our first date.
The days since then just come and go.
And sometimes I truly don't know
How this wonderful relationship can really be so.

And that it is just a dream to have you in my life.
To care for and about me for the rest of my life.
You showed concern for me when I was down
And helped me turn my life around.

So I want you to know that I truly do
Love, respect, and care for you.
Although circumstances in your life
Are bound to change,
Know that God's and my love remains.

And also understand this truth too:
If dreams were wishes and wishes came true,
I'd give all I own just to dream of you.

So, always remember that you have first priority
In importance, worthiness, and value to me
And that everyone else must accept that reality.

How Can I Do It?

How can a man get lucky enough
to find a lovely woman who actually
(really and truly) loves him?
At his age and stage of oldness
and for what he is, flaws and all?

How does a man show his gratitude
for a lovely woman who cares for him,
foibles and all?
How does a man thank
the person who makes his days
more interesting, yes, even exciting?

How does a man
repay those priceless gifts,
do justice to that love and caring?
I don't know. I wish that I did,
but I don't have a clue.
But I shall continue to try!

Clemency

Vindication is useful
A reprieve is wonderful
Forgiveness is sweet

A Special Anniversary

Today marks a special day for my friend and me.
For her, 40 years of life in the U.S.
following a very courageous and adventurous
voyage by merchant ship across the Atlantic Ocean,
alone and without relatives or friends, to a foreign land.

What could give a 25-year-old woman
the fearlessness, the boldness, the unmitigated daring,
the spirit, and self-confidence to undertake such a journey?
It takes more heart than most people could muster.
And that's exactly what she has in great measure:
intrepidity, resoluteness, and feistiness,
gifts that make her a very special person,
not only to her son and granddaughter.
but also to everyone she meets, including me.

But that is not the whole story,
and this is not the time or place to tell it.
So let me confine my words to describe
what her journey has meant to me.
She has given new meaning to my life,
a life that was torn asunder by the death of my wife.
Before I met her six years ago,
I was an emotional wreck, alone, lonely, and devastated.
Bur soon after meeting her again,
I was resurrected, renewed, and revitalized

She found a place in my life and heart
that I never knew existed.
Yet, it was there for four long years
until she filled it with care and a love
that was to be and is returned in kind.
For that, I shall be eternally grateful
That she made that pivotal journey in April 1965.

For Someone Special

I count the days that I have left
Realistically they are few.
Because I must make the most of them,
I pray that they involve you.

Your charm, warmth, and loveliness,
have captivated and beguiled me evermore

Although I know that I can never have you,
and I can accept that painful truth now.

That doesn't stop me from loving you
for your spell has me totally enthralled.

In Admiration

Knowing full well how difficult
the last few weeks have been for you,
how your emotional strength has been tested,
I am not only humbled but also inspired.
I count myself as one of the luckiest of men
to have you as my companion, friend, and lover.

As a consequence —
My need for you intensifies monthly
My respect for you grows weekly
My admiration for you increases daily
My affection for you deepens hourly
My appreciation of you heightens by the minute —
And my love for you multiplies exponentially.

What You Mean to Me

You brightened my life
When there was only darkness.
You restored my hopefulness
Where there was only despair.

You brought sunshine into my life
Where there were only clouds.
You gave me companionship
When there was only loneliness.

You renewed my optimism
When I had become cynical.
You made me smile and laugh
When I believed my grief was permanent.

You revived my ardor
When I thought I had lost it.
You renewed my vigor
When I believed it was irretrievable.

You mended my heart
When I knew it was beyond repair
But, most important of all,
You brought me love
When I needed it most.

I thank you for those
Priceless and indispensable gifts.

Quid Pro Quo

When you love someone
Your are blessed beyond belief
When love is returned.

About Us

Ours is a relationship deeply treasured
So rich, so sweet it can't be measured.
I look into your eyes and see affection there
Your tender heart is filled with care.
I'll watch over you as you do for me.
That is my promise, and it will always be.

So when trouble comes to pay you a call
I'll always be there to break your fall.
I'll protect you in every possible way,
Our bond, our love will survive ablaze
For we have ties that can't be broke
Ties that are as strong as the mighty oak.

Your Gifts to Me

When I awaken in the morning
You are the first thing I want to see.
When you are not there,
It makes the day very long for me.
I want to see you every minute as it comes
So that I can cherish each moment one by one.
You have brought much joy to me
An unexpected windfall, a wondrous gift
In the winter of my life

When I needed companionship and comfort,
You give them to me unconditionally
When I need love and caring,
You provide them wholeheartedly.
I want to spend the rest of my life with you
For you mean everything to me 'til the end of time
And I 'll love you completely
With this old heart of mine.

Remembering

It was only a few years ago
when we enjoyed good health
in our retirement on Cape Cod,
when the world seemed to be
completely oblivious to you and me.
Along the white Seagull Beach sand,
we walked together hand in hand.
Those days were ours to keep and share
Those days when you were always there
are gone forever, and I despair
But rest in peace beneath the enfolding earth,
beneath the marker that discloses your birth
and tells the world
that you were a loving mom, nanni. and wife.
So while you lie cradled deep in the sand,
I walk alone and seek your hand.

The Day You Left Me

The sun set early as expected in late October
But, it had been a beautiful Cape Cod day
And here was another one to enjoy.
I arose early, prepared for the day, and so did you
Late in the morning I went grocery shopping.
You helped me put the groceries away.
We then went our separate ways,
You reading in the living room.
I at work on the computer in my study.
All too soon, as if they knew you were leaving,
Clouds filled the sky, my study darkened, and I heard your cry
I called out asking what you needed.
I repeated the inquiry, but heard only a moan.
I dashed into the living room, took your hand,
looked into your eyes
And knew immediately that you were leaving me.

Forever Lovers and Friends

It happened on that special day

Some six-plus years ago

When God sent you my way.

So many friends had often called

But all too soon away they went away.

But I know that you were heavenly sent.

I know this because I prayed for you

Hoping I'd find a friend that's true.

I needed a special confidant and companion,

One I could hold within my heart,

I knew that person was you that very day

And right from the start

When we met at Way's Hallmark Shop.

I now have a very special friend

Who has helped me through life's strife

The person who has led me to that everlasting light —

The presence in my life of a forever friend

Who will be with me to the very end.

So shed no tears and never go away

Just promise me you'll always stay

For we have a very special bond

That will be with us to the very end

For we will forever remain lovers as well as friends.

That Special Day

The day you came into my life
The colors of sea and sky seemed brighter,
The sunlight radiated a warmer glow,
And the sea birds seemed to dance faster
On the breezes that softly did blow.

The fields seemed much greener.
And every flower with more color glowed
The day you came into my life,
and my love for you into my heart flowed.

The dolphins leaped a little bit higher,
As the gulls screeched their raucous symphony,
And all of God's wonderful creations,
Came forth for my eyes to see.
The beauty I had never noticed.
I viewed now with wondrous awe.

This was a day to remember
My step was stronger,
My heart felt younger
My mile was broader,
My mind was freer
The day you came into my life.

In the sea, the fields, and fauna,
Nature's power and God's love I saw.
My heart was so filled with joy
my soul within began to soar.
And my very being began to cry out,
"You are a woman to be adored!"

Relief

Lunch at the Back Room.
Always a wondrous event.
Communing with her.

You Are in My Heart

Stop agonizing, sweetheart,
everything will be all right
Just take my hand and hold it tight.
I will be your Guardian Angel,
I will be ever by your side.

So please don't weep.
For one so feminine and dainty,
you are also strong although small,
physically, mentally, and emotionally,
you have it all.

My arms long to hold you,
keeping you safe and warm,
closely enfolding you
protecting you from all harm.
The fiord that divides us
can easily be crossed,
but the bond between us,
can never be lost.

So please don't lament.
You'll always be with me.
Regardless of what others say,
you are in my heart always.
Why can't people understand
the way that I feel about you?

They just don't accept
what they can't explain
and that what I feel for you is real.

Although of different generations
deep inside us,
in our psyches and souls,
we are not different at all.
You are in my heart, always.

I don't listen to them,
and neither should you.
What do they know?
I need you and you need me,
to have and to hold.

People will understand in time.
When our fate befalls us,
and I am no longer with you,
you must be strong,
you've got to carry on.
Because you're in my heart, always.

Love Long Lost

By happenstance I met an old sweetheart today.
Her golden locks have turned to gray.
But the green of her eyes still holds a glow
And briefly tugged at my heart like so long ago.
Many years have passed since we said goodbye
Old reminiscences were opened, and I wanted to cry
We were so young, but the memories remain
And I remember them as if they happened yesterday
And the dreams and plans we shared and expected to stay.
Did she miss me while I was traveling over land and sea?
The world was my oyster, in its vastness and variety my joy
I had forgotten the love between a young girl and a callous boy
Now that I'm aged, less active, and frankly very old
Most of my memories, except these, have been told and retold
I have many descendants to carry my name,
but only the ashes remain of my lost flame.

Our Wedding

Realizing that short notices
demand quick decisions and actions.
Ignoring objections from our families,
my fiancé and I decided to marry.

Agreeing to set July 1, 1944 for the event,
just two days following my commissioning
as a Navy ensign in New York City on June 29th.
Receiving orders to ADCOMPHIBSPAC
in the Pacific Theater of war.

Noting the "short suspense" reporting date
of July 13 at the 12th Naval District in San Francisco
for transshipment to Hawaii.
Speculating about the type of ship assignment
I might receive.
Securing travel space in the U.S. Army
Transport Fred G. Ainsworth.

Learning that I was destined
for amphibious duty in the South Pacific.
Discovering that wedding planning was complicated
by the lack of parental or other funds and with no income
to spurge on an expensive wedding reception.

Adopting a practical solution:
holding the reception in the barn
at the bride's home and limiting the guest list
to relatives and friends living nearby.
Issuing phone invitations to grandparents,
aunts and uncles, and friends,
totaling about 25 people in all.
Providing only one adult beverage,
a keg of beer served in paper cups.

Hosting a modest repast
consisting of homemade tuna salad,
egg salad, and chicken salad sandwiches
served on paper plates
Featuring a small but decorated wedding cake
and an urn of hot coffee
Dancing to music provided by a record player
with the bride's younger brother
serving as the disc jockey.

Beginning the five-day honeymoon
with a bus ride to Boston
and a one-night stay at what is now
the Boston Park Plaza Hotel.
Clutching the magnificent sum of $55.00
— enough for one night at the hotel
(at a serviceman's rate) and a meal at a nearby cafeteria.

Traveling the next day on the T's Orange Line
to my sister's tiny four-room apartment
in the Mission Hill Project in Roxbury,
Accepting the use of my niece's bedroom
for the ensuing four nights.

Returning to my home in Leominster
where we stayed in the vacant third floor apartment
for the two days and nights remaining on my leave.
Being "caught in the act " on a sweltering summer afternoon
by my foster mother, along with a heartfelt "excuse me."

Diving on July 8 with my wife and best man
to Worcester where I boarded a troop train
for the four-day trip to the West Coast
to report for assignment.
Hiding my worries, fears, and tears
as I kissed my wife goodbye.
Learning later that she cried all the way home.

A Verse for You

Today, as on many days, I was alone
And I didn't have much to do.
So I decided to write some verse,
And somehow it was all about you.
I began by sitting in front of my computer,
But I didn't know what to write.
There were many things I needed to say,
But somehow they didn't come out right—
Like how your smile is contagious
And how much fun you are to be around.
Like all the times you have lifted my spirits
When I was feeling especially down.
So, I started talking about your son
And then your granddaughter too.
But there were so many nice things to say
That I didn't know where to start
Or even what to do.
So I decided simply to say to you —
"I thoroughly enjoy being with you
Not only because you're you,
But also because I love you too!"

If

If I were artist, I'd capture your beauty on canvas
If I were a singer, I'd sing love songs to you
If I were a builder, I'd build a castle for you
If I were a jeweler, I'd craft a special bracelet for you
If I were a horticulturist, I'd grow lovely flowers for you
If I were a psychic, I would tell you what the future holds
If I were a physician, I would keep you well forever
If I were an angel, I would watch over you day and night
But I'm not, so you'll have to settle for me as I am.

The Beautiful Lady in Red

On our most recent dinner date,
she wore red.
She was strikingly beautiful
my lady in red

So it's the year of the lady in red.
Throughout history, red has signaled
excitement, dynamism, danger, and sex.
And it signifies those things
better than any other color.

It's the most powerful color
psychologically and physiologically.
It's the color of kings
and religious royalty, the Cardinals,
and thought to be the color of life
and energy in the Chinese culture.

I'll never forget the image
Of her sitting across from me,
my lady in red.
I'm overjoyed that I had the good sense
to take four pictures of her,
although I told her at the time
that she would be beautiful
dressed in a burlap bag.
And she smiled at me!

Enthralled

This woman is cool
Because she is genuine
And very lovely

An Ode to a Special Person

You were sent to me from the start,
And never, ever shall we part.
For our love is here to stay
Not just because it is a special day.

I was lucky to find you
It was as unlikely as it was fortuitous
A wonderful and provident beneficence
A truly astonishing and remarkable blessing.

You are truly one of a kind
The very best woman that I could find.
So, if I could do it all over again,
You'd still be my choice, again and Amen!

So, here's to EMB, my companion and friend
Who loves to keep moving with the seasons
And pursues her avocation the daily numbers game
For the most obscure and arcane reasons.

I don't understand her fascination with numbers
Some people wager on them,
Most do calculations with them,
And others avoid anything to do with them

But, I love this woman
For a myriad of reasons
So, here's to many many more years with her,
While I ignore her wagering seasons.

One of a Kind

A great rarity —
An understanding woman —
and a gift from God

Friendship

True friends are rare gifts
They brace, sustain, and bless us
Therein lies their worth

The Gift of Friendship

The Lord knew that we needed
something more
than a burgeoning earth,
shimmering seas, and sunlit skies,
and so He sent us friends to love,
to lift our hearts and spirits high.

God chose to imbue love's
wondrous capacity
for pleasure and joy that never ends
by giving to our grateful hearts
the priceless and precious gift
of faithful friends.

So, give thanks to the Lord.
not just for the usual gifts of life and health,
but also for an irreplaceable largess
a capacity bestowed only to humans
for to love and be loved is to be twice blest.

Irreplaceable

A priceless present
A very friendly phone call
A loving promise

Norma

My long-time friend,
the lovely lady with the musical laugh,
peaches and cream complexion, radiant smile,
irrepressible sense of humor,
and upbeat demeanor.
She is a very bright woman,
intelligent and independent,
and with strongly held beliefs and opinions,
which she articulates and defends
effectively and vigorously.
An aficionado of classical music, especially opera,
and most especially Italian opera
in the *bel canto* tradition, and most specifically,
suitably, and appropriately,
a devotee of Vincenzo Bellini's *Norma*.
She is a giving person —
of her time, talents, and affection —
whether as a "big sister" to young women
in need of mentoring.
as an angel to older men and women
at the Quincy Hospice,
or going out of her way
to be a friendly and helpful neighbor.
A dancer par excellence,
expert at the waltz, polka,
cha cha cha, and rumba
and an accomplished belly dancer.
And she, like me, a cat lover.
ever a friend, protector, and companion to those
of the feline persuasion.
So Norma is a woman to be admired,
respected, and prized.
Although we have seen each other infrequently,
I consider myself fortunate
to be counted among her friends.

For a Grieving Friend

You are grieving, that I know
your anguish, pain, and sadness,
the endless sense of loss,
the heartache that will not go away —
the loss of your husband, J.
so cherished and adored.
Yes, you had some wonderful years together,
bringing children into the world,
a time of shared hopes and dreams,
of good times and challenging times,
the fate of all humans.
We know that J. has gone home to God,
that he is now in Heaven where he truly belongs.
Unprepared as you were, his passing was a harsh reality.
It was stunning in its impact,
so emotionally draining, so difficult to accept,
because your heart keeps telling you,
"Say it isn't so."
But it is now time to start the healing —
time to find peace, comfort, and solace,
and later on to reawaken and rejoice
in the beauty of the world that sustains you,
and keeps you whole and alive —

the gifts from God of your children,

your grandson, and your friends, old and new.

And remember this,

you all now have a special Guardian Angel,

one who watches over you every day

and remembers the love you gave him.

Know this about where J. now resides.

It's a place where he has been made whole,

where he is happy with his grandparents and the friends

who passed on before him.

And where one day you and your J. will meet again.

And he will take you in his arms and hold you tight,

never to be separated again.

To a Friend

If your road is long and twisting
And your heart is heavy too.
If you cannot see the ending
Because trouble blocks your view.
If clouds above are darker
As you climb each new hill.
Don't stop on your journey upward
Show your strength and your will.
Don't ever be a quitter
For around the next sharp bend,
You may come much closer
To finding a better way my friend.

For a New Senior Friend

Why do I admire you?
Let me enumerate the reasons.

You are an exemplary mother and grandmother
Kind and generous to your sons, daughters,
grandchildren. and friends
You are thoughtful,
Determined, unwavering, and indomitable.
You are considerate,
Prudent, focused, and solicitous.
You are bright,
Intelligent, clever, and quick.
You are buoyant,
Cheerful, sprightly, and upbeat.
You are caring,
Attentive, observant, and protective.
You are warm,
Amiable, genial, and openhearted.
You are loving,
Affectionate, feminine, and ardent.

So, I admire you because of those sterling qualities,
Gifts to everyone with whom you come in contact
that have made their lives better and happier.

But most of all I admire and respect you
Because you are you.

A Special Friend

You're my very life.
My lifeline and my friend.
I am so very grateful.

For a Lost Friend

A beautiful person in her own right,
she is SJ's mother,
the well-spring of her daughter's
outer loveliness of countenance and body
and the inner radiance of her mind and soul.
She calls her daughter "Janie Mae,"
a title of endearment allowed only to her
and no one else, including me.

J. is a warm, caring, wonderful woman.
She radiates compassion, consideration,
gentleness, kindness, and affection.
She is fun to be with and easy to chat with.
But, of much more importance to me,
she is a supportive listener and even provides
a shoulder to cry on when needed.

J. is remarkably candid and forthright.
She unerringly gets to the heart of an issue
and unhesitatingly states her position.
But she remains understanding and tolerant
of the perceptions and opinions of others
and never denigrates them for their beliefs.

J's voice is distinctive, immediately
recognizable because of its lyric tone
and its soft and engagingly breathy quality.
It is a joy to listen to her
and a delight to watch her eyes
and facial expressions as she speaks.
My guess is that she has a lovely singing voice.

J's love for SJ and concern for
her happiness and well being
are always evident.
In her words and actions she invariably shows
pride in her daughter, not only for her beauty,
but also for her accomplishments
over the years.
But the signs are also there
that her love is unconditional.

I would like to believe that, in the few hours
J. and I have been together,
much of that time spent with SJ,
we have become friends,
and that our friendship will flourish in the
months and years ahead.
I prayed daily for that outcome.
But it did not happen.

What Is a Friend?

The true value of a friend is immeasurable
It goes far beyond admiration and affection
It is something that is truly treasurable
Why?
Because a friend is cheerful and giving,
Kind, helpful and ever true.
He or she makes life worth living
Both for me, and for you.
Sincere, affable, and lovable
Doing good works every day
Bringing happiness and contentment to others
In the surest and best kind of way
So, here's a toast to friendship
A relationship that is here to stay

True Friends

There are no jewels more precious
Than the friends who have come my way.
My heart overflows with happiness
With the caring they share each day.

No matter if I'm depressed or blue,
Or feeling discouraged and low,
I can always count on their support
Until the good times flow.

Many are the faults I have,
but my friends don't seem to mind.
They know that I'm only human
and the good in me they look to find..

So, thank you Lord for my faithful friends,
Whose love is tested and true.
They walk with me on life's journey
And will always help me through.

Unparalleled

An ally is a boon
A good friend is a blessing
An old friend is rare

My Youngest Friend

A lovely little girl with a beguiling visage,
scintillating blue-green eyes, soft light hair,
and a delightful smile
that spreads sunshine all over a room.
Bright as a newly minted silver dollar
and with a sunny disposition to match,,
she easily wins the hearts of all she meets.

So, M is the epitome of a loving child.
truly a gift from God..
Her daddy, is handsome and charming,
and he obviously loves her to distraction.
To M, he is everything warm and loving,
and that is what he should be.
It is a virtue that is obvious to any observer,
but an essential characteristic of a good father.

Her Mommy is a beautiful woman,
a very special person for a lot of reasons.
Two of the most important:
She is a warm and caring wife, mother, and friend,
a joy to know and be with.
And, second, she has well-mannered and loving children,
traits that do not appear automatically —
they must be carefully nurtured..

I wish the best for M — a long, healthy, and happy life
and all of the things that will be useful to her
in the plan of God.
That is my heartfelt prayer.

My Newest Friend

She is an 11-year-old girl
with bright eyes, a sweet smile,
and beautiful auburn hair.
A soon-to-be sixth grader, she is the epitome
of brightness and openness.

She wears delightful braces on her teeth,
which are frequently displayed by constant smiles.
But, most of important of all,
she is warm, friendly, and trusting

Her name is Emily,
a charming name that suits her perfectly.
She is sometimes lonely,
and needs someone to talk with.

How do I know that?
Because she told me so
in a warm handwritten note
thanking me for doing just that.

And I was happy to have her
company. if only briefly.
I wonder why this little girl
should ever experience loneliness.
And I would do anything I could
to prevent its recurrence.

So Emily and I have become good friends.
We enjoy each other's company,
if only for a few minutes
when she comes riding by on her bicycle.

But meeting only on the front stoop
in plain view of passersby for reasons
that should be obvious.

I shall try to be ready to talk with her
any time she needs a listener.
And I stand ready to serve
as her stand-in grandfather figure
if that is what she wishes.

It would be good for Emily, a lovely young lady
— and good for me, a lonely old man.

Steadfast Friends

Steadfast friends, like genuine treasures
Aren't easy to find.
They're uncommon and they're priceless,
Each person one of a kind,

They're invariably caring and loving
and always ready to share
Your happiest moments,
As well as your deepest despair.

They're there when you need them.
They'll stand by your side,
No matter the weather,
In either low or high tide.

Steadfast friends are forever,
Whether near or apart —
Genuine treasures to cherish,
In one's spirit and in one's heart.

For My Friends' Engagement

God in His wisdom, splendor and grace
knew you would need each other
for the life challenges you face.
The times of joy that you will hold so dear
The times of sorrow that are certain to appear
The happiness on days that are clear
The trickle of a tear on days that you feel despair.
So, bind your hearts so that they can't part
Lock you hands and make your stand
Together you shall become as one
An enduring union to build your lives on.
God will be with you as you face each tomorrow
with peals of laughter and tears of sorrow
So when dark clouds begin to loom,
join your souls and stand unafraid.
For together there is nothing you cannot face
with God at your side with His comfort and grace.

Your Angel

My friend, God has given you an angel
He's watching you from above
Each and every day, he sends you all his love.
He's here to give you solace
And hope for each new day
As by your side and in your heart,
Forever he will stay.

My Friend, The Server

Blonde and green-eyed
with a peaches-and-cream complexion,
a shapely and womanly figure,
a demure and melodious voice,
and a warm and winning smile,
she is a feast for the eyes of all who meet her.

But, J is much more than a lovely woman.
She is the proud and loving mother
of three sons — Steven, Dylan, and Cameron.
And she is industrious and energetic.
She is not just good at her job.
She is a waitress par excellence.

Congenial, pleasant, and efficient,
she can handle a party of ten with ease
and, at the same time,
serve her usual number of assigned tables.

She has a prodigious memory.
For regular or frequent customers,
she remembers what they like,
their favorite libation,
even the kind of salad dressing they prefer.

But J. is much more than a great waitress.
She is a warm and caring woman,
a person who makes the day brighter,
and mitigates for an hour or so each week
the loneliness of an old widower
with her gentle smile and brief conversations.

Saying Goodbye

Saying goodbye is never easy
Tears fall freely as others stand by.
No one appreciates the pain inside
But you know you have to make it through.

As time goes by you will begin to heal
And remember the good times and never the bad
And the spirit of your closest friend
Will live forever in you.

As I awake and greet the dawn each day
My thoughts will be with you
And the good times we have shared
Each and every step of the way

I will feel your presence with me
And wish that I could touch you
And know that you are really there
To take my hand and walk with me.

Sometime in the days ahead
I'll understand what is to be
Why the things that overwhelm us
On days that are so dark we cannot see.

Those are the days when time stands still
And we ask God why it must be.
It's then that we hear a soft voice saying
"The sun will shine again, you'll see."

Nature

Wildlife, land, and sea
All parts of God's earthly plan
Prize it while you can

Seasons on Cape Cod

A flock of Canada geese soars by,
Seeking a feeding place;
Scrub oak trees shed their summer attire
And leave stark branches with empty space.

The blossoms on the roses fall
And scatter under the rail fence.
The long summer days will shorten soon
And only traces can be found
Of summer's verdant past.

When our world was green
and beach plums adorned the roadside
and cranberries ripened in the bogs.
Now fall will paint our piece of heaven
With warm and brilliant hues.

Off-white uncluttered beaches,
The sea a deeper blue.
And seasons pass in review,
In a reassuring and cyclical way
Each time of year a reason
For gratitude and joy.

A Perfect Cape Cod Day

Today is just too perfect
To pursue my ongoing projects and such.
Instead, it's a day for relaxing
And enjoying the sun's warm touch..
It's a day for doing nothing,
A time to think back
It's a day for counting blessings
And pleasures such as that.
It's a day to stroll the beach,
As gulls, terns, and hatchling plovers
Celebrate their release.
Precious moments such as these.
In the solitude of the evening
Dark shadows rise and fall,
As birds sing the benediction
And twilight comes to call.
This day brought many blessings
From dawn to setting sun.
And I praise the Lord
For all that He has done..

A Conundrum

When it's high tide here
People across Cape Cod bay
Are picking up shells

The Beach

I rode my bike to Smuggler's Beach today
And walked along the sand.
I picked up a handful and watched it trickle
Through the fingers of my hand.
I thought how insignificant each grain appears
When it's sitting all alone,
But when thousands are cemented together,
They become a mighty stone.
And then I watched the waves crashing
Against the manmade breakwater seawall jetty
And remembered how over time and many storms
They battered and demolished the protective shield.
And then I watched as the gulls swept down
And landed on the waves, bobbing up and down
As they surveyed their surroundings.

The Voice of the Ocean

I visit Thatchertown Beach often
For it opens out to the sea,
Where the rhythmical waves of the ocean
Deliver their melodies to me.
Whether it whispers on beaches
Or thunders on the jetty's stone
The powerful voice of the ocean
Proclaims a message all its own.
For it reveals the humbling power of God
As He subdues the ravaging storm
or proclaims the encompassing love of God
Gentle, tender, soothing, and warm.

Scrub Pines

Scrub pines bend their limbs
in deference to storms in winter.
Covered by wet snow,
they bow their heads in reverence.
Tomorrow's thaw will release their burden
Branches raised in pardon, all sins forgiven.

Autumn on Cape Cod

A wafting breeze, a golden haze,
A radiant sun on Autumn days.
A burst of light on distant swells,
As season's change brings morning chills.

Moored boats near the Bass River's mouth
Bob up and down with the tide
from the south.
And night birds flee in quivering flight
To find their shelter as it becomes light.

A church bell tolls the beginning of day
As sailors wend their way to the docks
To start another dangerous day.
Golden Autumn, my favorite season
September's gift, October's glow,
the time of year I love so.

A Fall Day

Sun shining brightly
Waves breaking serially
Seagulls complaining

Hurricane Bob

On Monday, August 19, 1991, Hurricane Bob.
a Category 2 storm, dropped in on Cape Cod and the Islands,
another uninvited guest like his cousins before him.
Showing little respect for the aesthetic value of our trees,
the sanctuary of our homes, a right to uninterrupted electrical
service, beautiful summer days, and undamaged property,
the storm provided wind speeds of 92 mile per hour,
3 1/2 inches of rain, and considerable damage.

Although not in the same league as the Hurricane of '38,
the State Police blocked the Sagamore and Bourne bridges
over the Cape Cod Canal
and sent motorists to evacuation centers at Camp Edwards..
Yarmouth was without power from Monday through Saturday,
Long enough to lose the food in the refrigerator and a freezer,
filled with lamb, beef, and chicken roasts,
corned beef, steaks, frozen meals and other foods—
which had to be thrown in the landfill.

We also lost several large trees,
one just missing my wife's car by inches,
and several sections of perimeter stockade fence.
Total damage for the town of Yarmouth was $1million,
and my share of that total exceeded $3,000.
The hurricane also earned me the wrath of my children
for not bringing their mother to a shelter.

Point and Counterpoint

A walk on the beach
A rewarding happening
Do it while you can
A sunless morning
Foghorns wailing mournfully
Seafarers beware

The Storm of the 20th Century

Arriving on a warm. muggy Indian summer day,
September 21, 1938,
the killer storm streaked up the East Coast.
with a freight-train speed of 60 miles-per-hour.
Aiming directly at New York and New England,
with wind speeds reaching 186 miles per hour.
Lacking hurricane reconnaissance aircraft,
weather satellites, and radar —
and the absence of reporting ships in the path of the storm,
the hurricane caught people completely unprepared.

Generating ocean waves of up to 80 feet high,
Tossing 20-ton breakwater boulders like pebbles,
Throwing large boats ashore,
Recarving shorelines,
Setting off devastating floods inland.
Killing 700 and seriously injuring 1,700 people,
Damaging more than 20,000 buildings,
Destroying 20,000 cars, trucks, and other vehicles,
Mowing down 250 million trees,
Obstructing all major highways,
Disrupting all communication lines,
Blocking streets with fallen trees, telephone poles.
and electrical and telephone wires,
the storm lasted 12 interminable hours.

Believing that the winds and flooding were local,
people looking for help, but none came.
Waiting two full days before the rest of the world
became aware of the terrible destruction.
But, I knew it because I experienced it!
Spending the initial minutes of the storm
picking up fallen apples for my Mom
until the limbs started breaking off the trees.

Watching the doors of the garage begin to bend inward.
Climbing the stairs to the third-floor tenement,
where I rode out the storm alone in the parlor.
Standing nervously by the window
overlooking Washington Street some 50 feet below,
while the house groaned and swayed like a ship at sea.
Fearing that the house would topple into the street.
Fortunately it did not

When the storm was over,
Venturing out into the street
Viewing the memorable devastation:
Trees uprooted, telephone poles downed, and cars crushed,
Electrical wires on the ground and everywhere.
Being trapped at home for several days after the storm
until city, telephone and electric company cleanup
and repair crews cleared the streets and restored services.

A Walk on Smuggler's Beach

I walked today on sand and smelled the beach
and felt the wind, and heard the roar of waves
breaking on the jetty
and tasted the salty air
and burned my face against the sun and wind
and swirling grains of sand.
I saw a small sea bass and a mid-size cod,
thrown by the waves into a tide pool
along with a horseshoe crab and a few hermit crabs.
The crabs were alive
but the fish, although glistening in the sunlight,
were both dead —from what I do not know
and cannot even guess.
But it seemed so sad, such a waste.
The echoes of my thoughts were quickly carried off
to memory by the wind.

Migration of the Birds

A magical time for birders.
Although I haven't earned the designation.
my lifelong interest in birds was kindled
by my high school biology teacher, Miss Burnham,
a dedicated naturalist and superb pedagogue.
September on Cape Cod,
that island-like peninsula that juts into the Atlantic,
marks the fall migration of birds of all persuasions.
The thrushes, warblers, orioles, and sandpipers,
among many others of our feathered friends,
fly from their summer in the Canadian provinces
to their winter Neotropical sanctum santorum,
singing their peeps, cirps, trills, tweets, and warbles
to bring joy and wonder
to native Cape Codders and "wash-a-shores" alike.
One of the mysteries of this annual pilgrimage
is the species of the unknown and identified calls
of the many small land birds
that make nocturnal choruses in flight using melodies
differing markedly from their daytime calls.
I still can't distinguish one from another,
although that doesn't stop me from enjoying
their harmonious serenades.
Many other species of birds are also on the move
—the ducks, geese, and loons, —
(although the Canada geese remain with us all winter)
the aerial hunters, the hawks and falcons, and other raptors,
and the massive flocks of tiny tree swallows
that gather en masse in uncountable numbers
— and make such charming call notes.
It is this time of the year, one of the "shoulder seasons,"
that makes Cape Cod a birder's paradise,
as well as a mystical place to live
and enjoy nature at its best.

War

Fear and loneliness
Bedlam, chaos, confusion
The hallmarks of war

A Day to Remember

Dawn of Sunday, December 7, 1941,
that heinous and reprehensible "day of infamy,"
when 200 carrier-borne "Zeros" and other aircraft
attacked Pearl Harbor and Hickham Field, Hawaii,
wounding 4,500 and killing 2,300 men and women.

The United States Fleet was grievously crippled.
Two battleships, the U.S.S. Arizona and Oklahoma were lost.
The U.S.S. California, West Virginia, Tennessee,
Maryland, and Pennsylvania were so severely damaged
that they were out of service for months to come.

I remember that day very clearly.
We had just finished our Sunday dinner
at 219 Washington Street, Leominster, Mass.
I was wiping the dishes in the kitchen
when the attack was announced on the radio.

I recall saying," Well, this is it! I'll be going to war."
Later that day, the Japanese declared war on the United States,
and the United States declared war on Japan December 8th.
But, for the moment, the war was pushed aside
as I tried to make a good start on my college education.

In preparation for the days and months ahead,
and determined to serve my country in a leadership position,
I began to build a foundation by taking additional courses
in meteorology, Morse code, navigation, and seamanship,
all useful subjects for a would-be Naval officer.

Several months later, I enlisted in the United States Navy
at the Office of Naval Officer Procurement in Boston
as a Seaman Recruit in the V-12 Officer Training Program,
the first step in my quest for a commission as an Ensign (DVG).

Navy Life

As one comes walking down Main Street
The first thing that catches his eye
are the signs portraying Navy life
and the "Good old Navy battle cry."

They show you scenes of battle
of Navy men so brave;
they show you all the glories
of the men who ride the waves.

"The Navy, ah, the Navy!
The challenge of it all.
It's wonderful; it's patriotic."
they say that so you'll fall for it and call.

And oh! Those handsome blue uniforms
that all the sailors wear.
They show those battle ribbons too.
But please, my friends, take care.

Don't be cajoled into enlisting,
And here's the reason why:
I joined the Navy, and now look at me.
I'm stranded high and dry.

I have yet to see the ocean.
I haven't been to sea.
Although the nautical rules of the road,
Have been well drilled into me.

I've studied mathematics
'til I looked like Cosine X.
I've got Naval history to study,
And Naval organization came next.

I've dealt with ship and aircraft recognition
until I was bleary-eyed with confusion.
And then pondered the rules of seamanship
including flag hoist exposition.

I'm told that I was very fortunate,
a very lucky guy.
I was in the Navy's V-12 program,
but hell, when did I give war a try?

So, listen my friends and take careful note:
The Navy is the right place
for someone who has lost his head
or is disoriented with undue haste.

Now I've given you fair warning,
and there's no good argument I have missed.
You ask me where I headed?
Why, of course I'm on my way to reenlist!

The Words of War

Combat, conflict, hostilities
Skirmish, battle, engagement
Fight, action, uprising, siege
Revolution, assault, donnybrook
Duel, confrontation, affray
Attack. showdown, resistance
Fray, brawl, strife, dissention
Warfare, clash, struggle, offensive
Contention, contest, encounter
Slaughter, carnage, massacre, melee
Bloodshed, butchery, PTS, TBI. holocaust
Destruction, devastation, IED, and death
Tough and graphic words
for a pernicious and chronicled reality.

Memories of War

Standing watch on the flying con in convoy.
Performing the duties of officer of the deck underway.
Listening to the wind howling through the halyards.
Hearing the clink of the flag clips on the ensign
Dinging against the flagstaff.

Feeling my heart fill with emotion.
Sailing thousands of miles away from home.
Transiting the immense Pacific Ocean.
Facing loneliness, homesickness, and death.
Experiencing total dependence on others.

Tolerating the lack of personal freedom.
Accepting the scarcity of privacy.
Stomaching the unappetizing food.
Withstanding the long days and nights
Wondering if the war would ever end.

Dreaming of a reunion with my wife.
Steaming toward the Philippine Islands.
Serving as part of a large armada of warships —
Imposing battleships, destroyers, and landing craft.
Voyaging their way to the Leyte invasion.

Obeying the klaxon's call to General Quarters.
Racing to my battle station on the forecastle.
Experiencing my first taste of combat action.
Feeling nervous, apprehensive, and uncertain.
Fearing failure, cowardice, disability. and death.

Recognizing the need to exemplify resolve and confidence.
Making the rounds of 40mm antiaircraft gun tubs
and 20 mm and 50 caliber machine guns around the foc'sle.
Shouting words of encouragement to my young sailors
over the deafening din and chaos of battle

Making repeated landings day and night.
Seeing star shells light up the beach and the sea around us.
Watching the red tracer rounds as they arced into the sky.
Hearing the train-roar of 16-inch, 14-inch, and smaller rounds
as they whooshed over from battleships, cruisers, and tin cans.

Enduring the continuing and frightening chaos of battle.
Striving to do the job I had been trained to do —
all the while striving to maintain my composure.
And from time to time remembering to hope and pray
That I would avoid injury and death.

Unloading tanks, trucks, troops, and supplies.
Surviving the Kamikazes, mortar fire, and snipers.
Retracting from the beaches successfully and unscathed.
Seeing the devastation sustained by adjoining landing craft.
Comprehending the destructive power of naval bombardment.

Praying for severely wounded soldiers, Marines, and sailors.
Needing desperately for the maiming and killing to stop.
Wondering if the war would ever end.
Dreaming of a reunion with my wife.
But, through it all,
Feeling pride in serving my country.

About Warfighters

They come in all races,
Sizes, genders, uniforms,
Some become heroes

Most were just young kids
Who had not seen much of life
But were shown hades

Vets of WW II
The greatest generation
A breed that's dying

The Civil War Tracey

Born to John and Bridget (Fahey) Tracey
in Rahan, Co. Galway, Ireland, March 1845.
John Tracey immigrated to Clinton, Mass working as a laborer.
Enlisted for three years in the 21st Regiment, Mass Volunteers,
in Worcester, Mass as a Private in the Infantry August 5, 1861.
His unit was sent to the Army of the Potomac where it engaged
in the battles of Roenoke Island, Newburn, and Camden. North
Carolina; 2nd Bull Run, Chantilly, South Mountain,
Fox's Gap, Antietam, Fredericksburg, VA,
and Knoxville Tennessee, and Covington, Kentucky.
After fighting in the Wilderness, May 6 1864 and Spotsylvania
May 12 and 18, and at Bethesda Church near Cold Harbor June
2, the unit was transferred to the front at Petersburg, VA and
participated in the assault of June 17, 1864. The 21st suffered
the loss of 31 officers and men: 4 killed or mortally wounded,
25 otherwise wounded and two taken prisoner.
Company B had one killed and two wounded,
including Private John Tracey,
who suffered a bullet wound to his shoulder.
John died of typhoid fever January 31, 1865, in Nashville, TN
While serving in the Quartermaster Department
John was my grand uncle — the brother of my grandfather,
Patrick Tracey

A Soldier's Final Sortie

Every soldier knows the time will arrive
To make that final sortie.
His family and friends bid fond goodbyes
And comrades wish him Godspeed.
He's serve his country, fought her wars,
Helped keep a nation free
And proudly did what he was asked
To preserve our liberty.
He did not face his journey
With apprehension, fear, or dread
Knowing that the loving arms of God
Is where this sortie led.
So, as the Flag was folded, Taps were played
And heart-felt Prayers were said,
This proud soldier
Was laid to his final rest.

Reville

"I can't get 'em up, I can't get 'em up, I can't get 'em up in the morning.
I can't get 'em up, I can't get 'em up, I can't get 'em up at all."
Is there a sound more annoying
than to hear the bugle screaming
when you're sound asleep and dreaming
of that very special dame?

Is there any more woeful feeling
than the one that comes a-stealing
when that strident, brassy pealing
calls our name?

For it's time to leave your sack now;
strip it down and turn it back now;
though the future might be black now;
Who's to blame?

Physical Training 0600

Hey jug heads! Form in line!

Do squat thrusts one hundred times!

Hup! Hup! Hup! Run in place!

On your backs! On your face!

Who complains of broken spines?

Jumping Jacks one thousand times!

Double-time it out and back,

Nineteen laps around the track!

He who faints, screams, or shrieks,

Gets the awkward squad for a least a week!

The Tree

In the Navy, there's a custom
that is quaintly called "The Tree,"
It's a devilish invention
of the old Academy.

You can climb it oh so simply.
No, it's not a chore at all.
But just wait until you're up there,
You can't jump off or even fall.

You just sit there on a limb, boys,
And you storm, sweat, and curse.
No liberty for you; sailor —you failed a test
Think now— the penalty could be worse.

Getting Letters

When you're far away from home
and you're feeling kind of blue,
when the world is topsy-turvy,
nothing sets just right with you.
You can sneer at all your troubles,
and your cares you never mind
when you've just received a letter
from the girl you left behind.

When the cook is downright fruity
and his biscuits never rise,
when he feeds you powdered eggs
for seventeen straight days,
you can lift your chin and whistle
and treat him reasonably kind,
if you've really gotten a letter
from the girl you left behind.

When the Captain's got a grouch on,
and has bawled you out for fair,
when the pesky Exec has dissed you,
which at home he wouldn't dare,
you can lift you chin and whistle
and that's easy as you will ever find,
if you've really received a letter
from the girl you left behind.

When a letter comes you grab it
right before the jealous guys
and you get an awesome vision
of the light that's in her eyes;
you can see her smile and dimples

and for other girls you're blind,
when you've really got a letter
from the girl you left behind.

Just a sheet or two of paper
with a purple stamp or two,
but it means the whole creation
to the heart and soul of you.
And you get to feeling pious
and you pray with an open mind
to the Great Almighty for a blessing
on the girl you left behind.

From Somewhere in the Pacific

In a faraway place I muse and dream
of future years with you
filled with laughter, joy, and love,
as we build our world anew.

Each passing day brings renewed hope
for victory, peace, and you.
in gratitude, let's pause this day
and say a prayer…..,we two.

For peace on earth, goodwill toward men
our prayer shall ever be,
and thanks to our God for America
where men and women are truly free.

The Navy

Navy was my choice.
An officer I would be
I achieved my goal.

September 11, 2001

A new world was born 9/11/01
another day "which will live in infamy."
Four separate attacks were perpetrated
on innocent Americans,
resulting in 3,000 dead or missing:
two attacks on the twin towers of the World Trade Center.
one on the Pentagon,
and one in the air over Pennsylvania.

And shortly after, the delivery of anthrax spores
in letters to the Congress, biological warfare,
resulting in the infection of several innocent people
and deaths of postal workers and others.
We were forced to believe what we cannot imagine.

We are at war, a different kind of war, but a war nonetheless.
We kept giving blood out of hope
that rescue workers would find people
whose lives it would save.
Workers continued to dig through ground zero
day after day and night after night
but with discouraging results — no one was found alive
after September 12th.

We and our country are changed forever.
We have been awakened to evil.
So, every day becomes a gift.
We are overwhelmed by the scent of a newborn,
the taste of a ripe apple,
the way the garden smells on a rainy day,
the sound of a bird song,
the roar of the sea as it crashes against the jetty.

Yes, we are confronted by America's greatest challenge.
its toughest test, one on which our survival as a nation rests.
Its name is terrorism, something even worse than Nazism
or other forms of totalitarianism.
It will test not only our resources but also our will,
our strength of character, our resolve.
We are at war! God help us all!

Landing Craft Lullaby

My sailor boy ain't got much rank,

but he cons a Landing Ship, Tank.

He "anchors away" to give 'em hell,

Leaning on the wheel of a Landing Craft,

Vehicles, Personnel.

Never fear he'll be capsized,

Bounding the main in a Landing Craft Mechanized.

If he should ever be attacked,

they'll come to the rescue in a

a Landing Craft Tracked.

If a big old whale rams him with its blubber,

he's save his life in a Landing Craft Rubber.

So hush now baby, don't you cry,

Daddy's coming home on an LCI.

The ship is really not a barge,

It's what is known as

a Landing Craft Infantry, Large.

Landing Ship Tanks (LST)

Created during World War II to support amphibious operations,
LSTs were fighting warships in every sense of the term.
Carrying tanks, trucks, pontoons, cargo, and troops,
landing them onto unimproved beachheads worldwide.
Proving the capabilities of amphibious vessels at Dunkirk in1941
Receiving Congressional authority for their construction in 1942 .
Building a total of 1,051 LSTs during World War II
Commissioned as 328 foot sea-going ships,
manned by the Alligator guys,
U.S. Navy and Coast Guard officers and men.
A complement of 8 – 10 officers and 100-115 enlisted men
and troop accommodations for approximately 140 personnel.
Featuring bow doors and ramps to unload troops and cargo,
a forward draft of fess than 4 feet for beaching, 10-knot speed,
a flat bottom, and equipped with 20 and 40 mm guns
and later, 50 caliber machine guns,
a 6-inch cannon and 40-mm twin mounts.
Seeing action in every theater of WW II
and receiving the second highest number of battle stars.
In addition to landing troops, vehicles, and supplies,
also served as torpedo boat tenders, battle damage repair ships,
mini-fixed-wing aircraft carriers, and hospital ships.
Leading the evacuation of 41,035 from Normandy beaches.
Involved in beachings in Sicily, Italy, Normandy, and So. France
Served in the Pacific island-hopping campaigns in the Solomons,
Guam, The Philippines, Marianas, Iwo Jima, and Okinawa,
Survivors of typhoons, attacks by kamikaze aircraft,
enemy subs, ocean mines, suicide swimmers,
and the dangers of mortar, machine gun, and sniper fire.
Providing amphibious landing and services during the
Occupation of Japan, the Korean War, Vietnam War, and
humanitarian services to Bangladesh, Operation Desert Shield,
Operation Desert Storm, and Operation Restore Hope.
LSTs were the large slow targets of amphibious warfare.
My ship, the LST 117, was called the Lucky 11 – 7.

Stepping Stones to Japan

Islands like Kwajalein, Saipan, and Wake
or Tarawa, Marcus, and Yap
sound or look strange to Americans
when they hear about them or see them on a map.

And then there's Engebi, Rota, the Bonins and Truk,
Majuro, Namus, and Palau,
Formosa, Kusaie, Eniwetok, and Roi,
plus Ponape, Guam, and Davao.

And let us not forget, New Guinea, Iwo Jima,
Leyte, Mindanao, and Okinawa
Manus Island, Guadacanal, Mios Woendi,
Owi, Padaidoes, Gavutu, Banika, Hollandia. and Samar.

These tongue-twisting, weird, unpronounceable spots
pointed the way that our forces would go
Through the skies, on the seas, over mountains and plains
to knock out our Nipponese foe.

An Ode to My Brother-in-Law
KIA Peliliu, 09/15/44

Of such that he was, there are few on Earth;

Of such that he is, there are few in Heaven.

And life is all the sweeter that he lived

And all that he loved, more sacred for his sake;

And Death is all the brighter because he died,

And Heaven is all the happier that he's there.

Ode to a Soldier

He as a man of many talents
An electronics buff extraordinaire,
A square dancer Debonair,
A tennis player better than fair,
A clock repairman beyond compare.

But those skills don't really show
The real man we all know.
He was a man with truly human qualities
Who had none of the common human frailties.
A modest man in every way,
Who showed concern for people every day.
A sensitive guy by his own admission,
Who was thoughtful of others regardless of position.
A warm and friendly man in all situations,
Who evoked respect and confidence
In times of trial and tribulation.
A gifted leader without flamboyance,
Whose ability to relate to others approached brilliance.

What better accolade exists
Than a simple statement that goes like this?
He was a soldier's soldier!

Written for my friend
Robert W. Lewis, Colonel, U.S. Army Intelligence
27 July 1974

About War

War is hell on earth
It destroys people and hope
It gives back nothing

Today's Ruthless Enemy

Osama bin Laden, The Taliban, Al-Qaeda,

the suicide bomber, the terrorist,

these are the enemy today.

Wearing no uniforms. planting IEDs,

they are men, women, even children,

indistinguishable from the general population.

They are unequalled in their brutality and barbarity

in any of America's wars

from the Revolution, through World Wars I and II,

to Vietnam and the Gulf War.

No American captured by these cold-blooded killers,

whether Soldier, Sailor, Marine, Airman.

or civilian employed by contractors

to serve in harm's way

has returned alive and unharmed.

When their remains have been found,

the condition of their bodies

attested to the terrible price

they paid for their patriotism, their heroism.

They were the victims of sadistic torture,

mutilation, even decapitation.

When faced by sadistic and inhuman adversaries,

surrender is not an option.

Life

Even with hard times
Life is always worth living
You get just one chance

Yesterday, Today, and Tomorrow

Yesterday is over, finished.

We cannot go there again

although the memories still linger

and there is much to savor —

especially the events of the last year.

And those memories are attributable

in great measure to EMB.

Now, today has just begun —

a day in the second month of the New Year—

and it's St. Valentine's Day.

What can we do for the dozen hours

we have at our disposal?

What new experiences can we enjoy today?

Will they be useful?

Will they be worth remembering —

and possibly written about later in verse?

Again, they will depend in large part

on my best friend and loving companion, EMB.

-And now, most important of all,

What about tomorrow?

What can we look forward to?

What possibilities and opportunities do it,

and the unknown number of days that follow,

offer to her and me?

Will they really change anything in our lives?

Will we have new experiences

that will make a difference in our universe?

So, we must not forget the past lest we have no future.

But that will happen only if we have learned

from our yesterday and all the yesterdays before it.

We must pursue a new lesson today,

one that can change our tomorrows for the better.

Whether they bring joy or sorrow

depends on you, my EMB, and me.

Musings

The wonder of life
is to love, not to be loved,
to give, not to receive,
to serve, not to be served;
to be a strong support
to another in time of need,
to be a tower of strength
to any person in
a crisis of adversity.
This is to know
the wonder of life.

Living on Borrowed Time

In the winter of your life,
you realize that you're living on
borrowed time.
Whose time, you don't know.
It could be your grandfather's
or your mother's or your father's,
or even your sisters and your brother's.
But no matter from whence it comes,
that time is still borrowed
and must be paid back
at some future time.

On Aging (Reluctantly?)

Aging gracefully is not easy,
It even makes you feel quite woozy.
Sit on the edge of a bed before standing up
Am I going to bed or just getting up?
look in the mirror and get a shock
The mirror I bought didn't have those age spots.
Go into a room to get an item,
but when you get there you've already forgotten.
My kitchen is often a disaster,
however in there I'm invariably the master.
I often take twice as many steps as I need to.
simply because I forgot what I was about to do.
So, I smirk and take it all with grin,
I'm in exceptionally good shape
for the shape that I'm in.
Aging is simply a matter of how you take it,
if your health is good you can always make it.
Do a little every day even if it's just a bit,
and if it hurts a little, show a little grit.
It also feels so good when you can finally quit.

Thoughts on Our 5th Anniversary

Remembering clearly the years gone by.
Knowing confidently that they have been precious.
Needing profoundly to say something meaningful.
Bemoaning fervently my deficiencies in articulating emotions.
Striving diligently to find the right words.
Facing fearfully the prospect of failure to find them.
Recalling pleasurably the days and evenings on Cape
And reprising fondly our transcontinental excursions.

Thinking earnestly about our relationship.
Enjoying thoroughly our closeness.
Delighting in your energy, alertness, and vibrancy.
Savoring your spontaneity, openness, and generosity.
Admiring your tenaciousness, inquisitiveness, and outspokenness.
Relishing your femininity, seductiveness, and sensuality.
Persevering religiously to retain your trust and affection.
Avoiding meticulously disputes and confrontation.

Striving desperately to be supportive and helpful.
Encouraging resolutely changes that promise to be beneficial.
Fostering meticulously compromise and mutual respect.
Realizing fully that we share many things.
Wanting desperately to let you know how much you mean to me.

But, most of all
Wisely and prayerfully accepting our need for each other.
And adhering faithfully to the words and actions
That will enduringly strengthen our love
And unfailingly and perpetually keep us together.

Why Do I Cry?

I'm a "big boy" now,
approaching 86 years old.
I'll never forget
my foster father's admonition
That "big boys don't cry."
Yet, over those many years
I have had plenty of reasons for crying.
I cried when I was hurt physically,
whether due to a fall, a punch, or a birching,.
I cried when I was wounded emotionally
whether due to a death in the family,
unkind words, cruel or undeserved punishment.
I cried when I was injured spiritually
whether due to unwarranted accusations,
uncalled-for aspersions, or slanderous remarks.
From my sister: I was ugly
and could never get a pretty girl.
To my foster father: I was stupid,
a loser who would never amount to anything.
To my fiancé's aunt: I was a nobody
because I didn't even have my own name
(I was adopted).
But, I'm not looking for sympathy.
I survived the tears and the anguish.
And found happiness with
my beautiful wife, six extraordinary children.
twelve wonderful grandchildren,
and a truly rewarding career.

About Haiku

Haiku is tricky
And very difficult too
I craft it anyway

The Weekend Short-Order Cook

In the 60s and 70s on Richardson Drive
I developed my skills as a breakfast
short-order cook on Saturdays and Sundays
preparing large quantities of scrambled
eggs, bacon, and toast
for three to four of my teenage children
and their guests for a day, a weekend, or longer.

The menu never varied, nor did the quantity
— orange or grapefruit juice, a large pot of coffee,
two pounds of bacon, two dozen eggs,
and a loaf or more of toast —
served at the seven-foot picnic-style kitchen table
with attached seats. made by my friend Ernie Lowe and me.
Our most frequent guests were Susie Gurley, Betsy Gurley,
Ski, the nurse in training, Jimmy, Maura's friend,

We never minded the time, effort, or expense involved
because we were privy to their conversations,
and therefore knew
that our kids were not recovering
from a bad night.
It was a worthwhile investment.
One that saved my wife and me
much worry and heartache.

An Admission

Most of the boldness
That I appear to possess
Is only false show

There's a Reason

For every gift that we have received,
For every joy that we have shared....
There's a reason.
For every love that we have received
For every sign of caring we have seen....
There's a reason.

For every enchantment that we have experienced,
For every delight that we have embraced....
There's a reason.
For every elation that we have known,
For every bliss that we have felt....
There's a reason.
For every pain that we must bear,
For every burden, every care....
There's a reason.
For every grief that bows the head,
For every teardrop that is shed....
There's a reason.
For every hurt, for every slight,
For every lonely, anguish-filled night....
There's a reason.
But if we trust in God, as we should,
it will all work out for our good....
He knows the reason.

A Sad Truth

Although I have no regrets
I could have lived differently
If I cared less about what others thought

Life's Mysteries and Wonders

I've often wondered
what got me started as a writer.
As a student, writing was a travail for me.
It remains a mystery to me
why I chose to make it an important,
even necessary, part of my life.
By nature, I am truly a people person,
although I like to limit my contacts with people
to a very few at one time.
However, writing is a solitary occupation.
It separates one from people
because it demands silence
and time alone with your thoughts.
As a writer, I have found that what is wonderful
is not so much producing an article,
a piece of verse, or even a book,
but all the little mysteries
that accompany the writing venture.
Even after finishing a book,
I've been perplexed as to why I was attracted
to one subject and not to another.

It's True!

I'm a self-made man
Who owes his lack of wealth and status
Only to himself
The opportunities were often there
But there were reasons why they were rejected
Most related to family
But, I have no regrets
M life has been rewarding
And I have been blessed.

What's in a Name?

In the course of a lifetime, everyone, including me,

has several names: family names, given names, middle names,

nicknames, pet names, diminutives, sobriquets,

monikers, handles, pen names, or aliases.

People are also addressed in person or in writing

by honorifics and titles, many of which indicate prestige,

importance, respect, esteem, even celebrity.

Still others indicate disrespect, or are simply put downs, slurs,

in the parlance of today, disses

—epithets, ridicule, or contempt.

Here are some of the names

I have been given, earned, or awarded

and the context in which they were used.

As a baby I was called "Baby,"

"Little Brother, " and "Little Billy."

As a youngster in grammar school,

I was known as ""Billy," "William,"

"Shorty," and "Willie."

In high school and college, I was called "William," "Bill,"

and "Mr. Tracey," a "grammar master,"

and when elected a class officer, as "Mr. President."

In the Navy, I was first "Seaman Recruit Tracey,"

then Seaman Apprentice Tracey," next "Midshipman Tracey,"

and upon commissioning, "Ensign Tracey," and with succeeding
promotions, to "Lieutenant (jg) Tracey," "Lieutenant Tracey,"
"Lieutenant Commander Tracey,"
and finally, "Commander Tracey."
I was alternatively called "Mr. Tracey" or "Sir" in the grades of
Midshipman, "Ensign," and " Lieutenant,".
As a college teacher, I was called sequentially, "Instructor
Tracey," "Professor Tracey," or "Mr. Tracey,"
and following receipt of my doctorate,
I became "Doctor Tracey."
When I worked for the Army,
I was invariably addressed in person or in
writing as "Doctor Tracey" by all ranks from Private to Sergeant
Major, and from Warrant Officer and Lieutenant to Four Star
General — even by the Army Chief of Staff and Assistant
Secretaries of Defense. I held one other title when I served as a
member of the Commission on Vocational,
Technical Career Institutions, NEAS&C — Commissioner.
But my family had the greatest number of names for me:
My wife called me Bill and addressed her letters to me as
"My Darling Bill," or "Honey"; my children invariably
called me "Daddy" and when they were older, "Dad"; my
granddaughter Tamra gave me the
name "Poppi" when I preferred to be called "Grandfather,"

and she won that contest;

most of my daughters-in-law called me "Dad";

the exception was Lina, who always called me "Abuelo,"

My sons-in-law call me "Bill."

My great granddaughters are likely to call me "Great Poppi,"

All of my nieces and nephews call me "Uncle Bill."

I'm sure that there were many other names given to me by

students, subordinates, and associates, some of which would

probably be unprintable.

At Christmas

When Christmas comes, I always think
of the family and friends that I have known,
whose tenderness and kindness touched my life
in ways that were theirs alone.
Family and friends whose caring and loving
drove the cold and loneliness away.
and always brought me happiness
on every Christmas Day.

When Christmas comes, I always take
a walk down memory lane,
and all the joys I used to know
warm my heart again.
And it's times like this I feel
God's blessings through and through,
not just because it's Christmas,
but because of a wonderful woman like you.
I love you!

Speculating about a Relationship

Was I for a time just an interesting diversion?
And then did I increasingly become a burden?
Yet, I was very serious about her as a companion
and asked for more of her time and affection
than she apparently was willing to give.
Has she since been trying to "wean me away"
by ignoring my communications
and failing to acknowledge my gifts and affection?

If that be the case,
and my speculation is correct,
I can now only wish
that a more straight-forward approach
had been taken to end the relationship.

She should have told me
that our friendship had no future
and that it would be best for us both
if I just disappeared and got out of her life.
Although that would have been a hurtful solution,
it would ultimately have been much kinder
than the "slow death by neglect"
that I endured for far too long.

An Axiom

Very few people do
Anything creative
After the age of 40
The reason:
Very few people do
Anything creative before
The age of 40.

Soups, Stews, and Chowders

When prepared properly
using no salt, lean meat,
vegetables, or reduced-fat milk
they are low in calories, the perfect food.
Meat-based concoctions are
hearty and satisfying, zesty and robust.
Poultry-based blends are
succulent and tasty, savory and appetizing.
Vegetable-based mixtures are
flavorful and healthy, pleasing and wholesome.
Seafood-based combinations are
delicious and nutritious, ambrosial and luscious.
Creamed preparations are
filling and nourishing, rich and comforting.
Fruit mixes are
refreshing and delectable, gourmet and heavenly.
So enjoy soups, stews, and chowders,
They are easy to make,
sure to please your guests and your palate
... and they are good for you.

Unforgettable Women

Mrs. Harry B. (Ruth) Smith,
next door neighbor, nurse, and mother of my friend, Harry.
A beautiful woman, who always treated me as someone special!
Mrs. Manning (Elizabeth) Morrill,
my high school English teacher,
the first person to insist that I apply for college entrance!
All of the piece-working sewing machine women
on the 3rd floor of the Cluett, Peabody Company, Inc.
Arrow Shirt factory in Leominster
who teased me unmercifully —the 17 year old "gofer"
and the only male on that floor—
and took up a collection on my last day of work
to pay my freshman year tuition at Fitchburg State College.

Past Failures

Over failures past we should not grieve.

Things behind us we should forever leave

Forget the past and look ahead.

Yesterday's mistakes are now dead.

About tomorrow, we should not agonize

Nor should we fear what lies ahead.

For half the troubles we surmise

are really blessings in disguise.

Tomorrow will soon come our way

Today will soon be yesterday

This day is ours to make or impair.

Let's face today without a care.

The Gift of a Smile

A smile is a gift you give yourself

by giving it away

because it comes right back to you

in a caring and friendly way

A smile can say a lot without using words

wherever you may be,

in open, unpretentious ways

that anyone can see.
A smile shows you understand
when a heart is filled with care
for it projects compassion
and relieves the mood of despair.
A smile produces a joyous bond
that binds us one and all
with strands of human kindness
no matter where they fall.
A smile's a flower that when returned
becomes a full bouquet.
A smile's a gift you give yourself
by giving it away

The Blessing of Time

Time is a blessing,
depending on how you use it.
You can make it productive
or you can easily abuse it
Time is a treasure.
so preserve it in your soul.
Keep all of its spending,
completely within your control.

Living Day by Day

I'm contented with this day,
For this near-springtime of the year,
When the days become longer
and the nights shorter.
For spring invigorates my soul
And brings such beauty near.

The days I must live one at a time
with the beauty of the Cape all around,
for one and all to enjoy
without a price to pay for its premiums.
To share in so much pleasure
in fragrances and nature's sounds.

For me, each spring is better than the last;
I feel this deep within.
Each day is fresh and new and bright...
So let each day begin.
I try to enjoy them to the fullest
despite the loneliness I must endure
and tough it out again and again.

Why?

Why paint dead flowers?
Or apples, grapes, and onions?
Girls are prettier!

Some read every line
I omit the boring stuff
Parts that others skip

Fame is so fleeting.
You are on top one bright day
And vanquished the next

My Plea

Do something today that tomorrow
will prove to be really worthwhile.
Help me to conquer sorrow
and greet each new day with a smile.

For only through kindness and giving
of service and friendship and cheer,
do we learn the pure joy of living
and find heaven's happiness here.
If you want to make a difference
in another person's life,
Be helpful when you're needed,
Let him know you care.

Be patient and forgiving.
Even when hurts are hard to endure.
Doing so will make you light-hearted
and for him make life worthwhile.

The Highroad

I ask much of me
The price is always costly
But I must pay it

Verse that I create
I must fully understand
Otherwise it means naught

What I can't create
I really don't understand
Insight is the key

Thank God, I'm Still Here!

I thank God I'm still alive..
that the skies are still blue,
that a new day dawns
for me and for you.!

The sunlight glistens
on the beach and the sea,
and the cardinal sings
to his mate and to me;
and my whole world shimmers
with extraordinary jollity.

I know that there are heartaches,
dilemmas and obstacles,
problems, and challenges
in this world full of strife.
.but I still thank the good Lord
just for giving me long life.

Peggy and Polly's Song

This is the song my sisters sang:

I have a dear little dolly,
She has eyes of gray-blue,
She can open and shut them,
And she smiles at me too.

In the morning I dress her,
And we go out to play,
But I love best to hold her
At the close of each day.

New Beginnings

Every day offers a new beginning,
for every morning the world is made new.
So if you are weary of sadness and wrongdoing,
there is hope, not only for me but also for you.
All things of yesterday are past and over
your work is done and your tears have been shed,
yesterday's mistakes let today cover over,
healed with the balm the night has dispensed.
Every day offers a fresh beginning.
Allow your heart to listen to the joyful refrain.
In spite of your guilt, even sinning,
you can take heart and begin again.

So, with resolute heart and true,
go forward on your way.
You have the inner strength to do
the tasks that come your way.
Daily may this thought
come repeatedly to your mind and soul,
"I can make my way because I ought,
and with God's help, I will."

Random Thoughts

It gives me great joy
To know that I can write words
That make people think

Find your special Muse
By random rumination
It only takes time

The Fate of a Published Poem

After you write a poem
it no longer belongs to you,
like the bottles
with notes from children,
released into the ocean
off Smuggler's Beach.
There's no knowing where
the notes will land.
Some may travel great distances,
and crash on the breakwaters
or cliffs of the coasts of
Ireland and England
or the beaches of Normandy.
Some few may be retrieved
by beach walkers along those shores.
But most, like my verse,
will never be heard from again.
They are no longer yours.

Trusting You

I trusted you
and you misled me.
I cared for you
and you let me down.
I loved you
and you abandoned me
Now I'm alone
and wishing that you were back
So, although I must leave you,
I will always love you

My Favorite Server

I don't think you know
that I write verse.
It's true.
So, I've written a little sample,
just for you.
I trust that you won't misinterpret
my motives or intentions
for they are completely honorable
and totally respectable.
I thank you for your kindness
toward a lonely old man
with a penchant for a very dry Martini,
dips and crackers
with a dash of Tobasco,
followed by roast turkey
with a side of extra gravy.
And let's not forget
his unfilled craving
for mashed butternut squash,
instead of the green peas
that the chef insists on serving.
And topping everything off
with grapenut pudding and black Decaf,
a weekly ritual that makes my friends laugh.

P.S. I have probably misspelled one or more
of your sons' names
in an earlier bit of doggerel
If so, .and if you would like another copy
with the names spelled correctly,
—just make the corrections
in pencil or ink on this copy,
and I'll make a new copy.
It's all on my computer!

Priceless Treasures

All too often we overlook
life's most important riches.
the inheritance common to all humans.
For in everyone's life there are treasures
more precious than diamonds or gold.
And none of these priceless treasures
can ever be bought or sold.
Whether we live on the plains,
the mountains, or near the sea,
there are joyful vistas
made just for you and me.
The beauty that surrounds us
along life's thoroughfare
are treasured gifts from God
for all of us to share.
The delicate ministrations of a mother,
the affection of a caring father,
the tender love of a spouse,
the sound of children's laughter,
the helpfulness of good and faithful friends.
are treasures that we should cherish
until our life's journey ends.
So all of these gifts from God
so critical to our well-being,
to our satisfaction with the hand
we have been dealt,
are more precious than diamonds or gold.
For the beauty of our land
and the love of our parents,
spouse, children, and friends
can never be bought or sold.

On the Wall of My Study

Among the framed diplomas, degrees,
certificates, awards, and military service medals,
on the walls of my study and the adjoining dining room,
there are many photos of myself,
both in and out of uniform,
as well as persons who were important in my life —
my mother, my wife, my children,
my grandchildren, and my great grandchildren,
the latter three categories totaling 20 souls.
But there is a photo of two young men,
one in the uniform of an Army corporal
and the other of a Navy apprentice seaman.
They are my brother Jim, age 24, and me, age 19.
The photo was taken when we were both on leave at home
during World War II, a few short weeks before Jim shipped out
to Italy and later to Liberia, Africa to serve in the Air Corps,
and I left for Midshipmen's School for officer training,
commissioning as a Navy ensign, and subsequent assignment
to a Landing Ship Tank in the Pacific Theater of operations.
We corresponded during the next two years whenever we could.
Two years later, we were reunited, and for the remaining years
of his life, we were the best and closest of friends.
I miss him terribly.

That's Me

Persistence personified
Compulsively focused
Romantically inclined
Resolutely honest
Intensely loyal
Unremittingly tenacious
Emotionally vulnerable
Invariably naive
Unfailingly loving

The Value of Verse

Verse speaks to us about life,
of soothing comfort or corrosive strife,
heartache etched deep or the joys of life,
barren horizons or majestic heights.
Verses teach us as we read
about triumphant victories or trying defeats.
To promising sanctuaries they often lead,
or cheerless voyages, yet we still proceed.
If you examine verse, it brings into view
bygone times or vistas new.
Listening to the hardships of a few
or seeing heartfelt wishes come true.
Learning of legends in images deep,
the incredible itineraries individuals keep,
verdant woodlands where willows weep,
secluded places where all may sleep.
Revealing secrets never before shared
or meeting heroes once unknown.
We travel far, it brings us home
that wondrous verse we call a poem.

The Gift of Time

Yesterday is but a memory.
Tomorrow is an uncertainty.
Today is an opportunity.
Don't squander the chance
to reach out to someone
who badly needs friendship,
if not romance.
Plan now to grant his yearning
to spend quality time
with a lady who is amenable,
so warm and compatible,
so upbeat and congenial.
Visit his piece of the Cape..
Enjoy the sunlit beaches.
the windswept dunes,
the thundering surf
as it pounds the jetty's outer reaches.
Share the cooking duties,
making a tossed salad,
boiled lobster with melted butter,
accompanied by French bread
and a good quality Merlot
to make your heart flutter.
Listen to his stories,
relieve his cares,
and put to rest his lonely tears.
So, don't put off until tomorrow
what you can do today.
The gift of time is far too precious
to waste a single day.

A Reality

In the business world
Survival of the fittest
Is today's end game

On Aging

The so-called golden years
are not all they're cracked up to be.
Finding out that you
can't do many of the things
you have always done effortlessly —
climbing a ladder, or scaling a wall,
jumping a fence, running an eight-minute mile.
memorizing a poem,
remembering a name, or
recalling the precise word you need
to express yourself clearly.
Yes, there are bright spots, too.
things you can do even better
than when you were young
remembering your childhood and youth,
loving your spouse, children, and grandchildren,
cooking a full meal, writing a bit of verse
all made possible by your length of years,
your life experiences.
So, let us make the most of the tradeoffs
and enjoy what remains of our time here.

Just Do It!

Make visible what
Without you might never exist

So, do it right now!

You have shelved dreams
Unfulfilled vows and pledges
Make them happen now!

A Life Restored

High up in my maple tree,
So strong, so solid,
So unlike me at this time of my life.
I am old and weak
Emotionally distraught.
Nestled in giant branches, I am being held
Like I am never held by anyone any more.
High above everyone, I'm safe,
Without care, free to dream
And plan the short life that lies ahead.
Seventy years fly by like the autumn leaves
Being blown about by the wind,
All of my plans, schemes, hopes
And dreams, many of them achieved…
Wins and losses, the up side and the downside.
I was happy with my life
after a difficult childhood and adolescence.
I found joy in my marriage,
my children and grandchildren
and fulfillment in my work and writing.
I lived my life like a prayer,
Learning from my wife
To "let go of the trivial
And let God take care of the critical."
My focus was on quality,
Rather than on quantity, on satisfaction,
Rather than on money.
For five long years I was alone
And had lost my life's compass.
I needed a love in my life and finally found one.
She truly shares my feelings,
So I am no longer desolate, discouraged, and heartbroken
Things are different. My heart is mended.
My life is restored!

Feelings and Fears

Doubts and guilt on sand are built.
Tears and jeers, feelings and fears.
She is not here, but gone away
She is not here, she could not stay.
I am so lonely even in a crowd,
I cry for help. I am not too proud.
But no one hears. Are they perverse?
I need help. I need an embrace.
I need the strength of Hercules,
help from Above.
Or I'll become listless, unfeeling,
if nothing, no one offers me consolation.
Lord, where are you?
Have you left me alone to weep 'til the day
when I, too, go death's way?
No, thank God,
I will never be left to fight alone,
For the Light-of-the-World is here,
My Father is always near.

Maxims in Haiku

A "beautiful man"
Is an anachronism.
Men can be "handsome"
A very plain girl
Oftentimes becomes the bride
Of a handsome man
Loving is a gift
Receiving love a blessing
Let us be grateful

Susie, the Ideal Waitress

Susie, the pretty girl
with the shiny black hair
and the waist-length ponytail,
the girl with the warm smile
and the genial presence.
She makes customers feel special
just by the way
she greets and serves them.

I can't describe graciousness,
but I see it in her bearing.
I can't describe her charm,
but I see it in her demeanor.
I can't describe the kindness,
but I see it in her eyes.

I can't describe the friendliness,
but I hear it in her voice.
But can anyone say why
there's magic in the sky?
Or explain why every river
runs into the sea?

No more can I explain why
Susie has made a friend of me.
But knowing she's so likable
and the reason for this verse too,
I can't say why I admire her so much,
it's enough to know I do.

The Mind

Thoughts inside one's mind
Aren't always as crystal clear
As we'd like them to be

Friday Nite Dance

At Dolly McDaid's School of Ballroom Dancing
on North Street, just beyond the Teachers College.
At first, the price of admission, fifty cents,
but later, free to Speed and me as Dolly's dance partners
demonstrating the new dances for the other patrons.

We learned by watching Dolly and her husband,
Warren, demonstrate the new step,
practicing the step with Dolly,
and then teaching it to one of the "paying" girls.
After the lesson, there was free "slow dancing"
until nine P.M.—
and the opportunities afforded by the close contact
to arrange for a date after the dancing school closed
or at some later date.

We learned the Two-step and the Foxtrot
the Waltz and the Polka, Square Dancing,
the Rumba and the Cha Cha Cha
the Quickstep and the Jitterbug
and then the most difficult of all, the Tango.
My dancing partners, and later my dates,
included cute little blonde and blue eyed Jean,
captivating brunette and brown eyed Lucille,
seductive red head and bombshell Mary.
and graceful and comely Barbara,
who later married one of my students
and later a subordinate civilian employee and friend,
World War II Marine, Joe.

Those were the happy days,
driving around in Mr. C's 1933
Cadillac touring car or my Pop's 1936 Pontiac.

The Saddest Time of the Year

The Christmas Season, the Holidays,
a time for giving and loving,
a time for prayer and thanksgiving,
a time for remembering.

For me, Christmas has often brought sadness,
melancholy, nostalgia, and depression.
I know not why I have been so afflicted,
both as a child and adolescent,
and the anguish never completely disappeared,
even when I still had the love of my life
and was surrounded by my children.

Now, in the twilight of my existence,
I am again despondent,
although my life has been brightened
by a new love, a warm and wonderful woman.
With her help, comfort, and support
I now hope to avoid the feelings of hopelessness
that have plagued
me for all too many years.

Do I dare to be happy and joyful this year?
I shall try my very best.

White Christmas

A cold and gray day,
rain drumming on the windows —
a time for repose
I prefer a good snowstorm
with big, glistening snowflakes
blanketing the ground

The Evening Meal

The place: West Townsend, weekdays
The time: between six and six-thirty p.m.
The seating: the 7-foot maple-finished picnic table
With seats attached,
Six kids and guests on each side,
Mom at one end and Dad at the other.

First guest, a roomer for several years,
Julie (Country) D,
a teacher at Ashby Elementary School
And later, redheaded roomer, Ellen W.,
a music teacher turned primary grade teacher in Ashby.

The setting: no television and no phone calls.
The agenda: what happened in everyone's day
school, work, friends, or current events.
The rule: keep conversation positive, no arguing,
no fighting, allow everyone a chance to speak.

The menu: plain but nourishing and tasty,
shepherd's pie, chicken pie, boiled spare ribs,
creamed salmon and peas, Swedish meat balls,
baked beans and frankfurters, spaghetti and meat balls,
beef stew, Finnish cabbage rolls, stewed chicken,
chicken á la king, fish chowder, corned beef and cabbage.
stuffed green peppers, meat loaf, macaroni and cheese,
tuna casserole, or, occasionally, pot roast of beef.

And, on Sundays, roast stuffed chicken or turkey
with mashed potatoes, gravy, fresh vegetables.
and pie for desert. usually apple.
Bon appétit!

A Plea for Compassion

I am desolated,
abandoned and forsaken,
depressed and dejected.
I am heartbroken.
My dear friend,
Please pardon me.

Although you have been wronged
and are deeply hurt as a consequence,
do what your warm and caring heart
has always asked,
and you have never failed to do.
Please pardon me.
Indignation, resentment, and anger
keep wounds open.
Only forgiveness heals.
Never throw genuine friendship away.
It's too precious, too special, too rare.
Please pardon me.

More About Women

A charming woman
Is a priceless gift from God
For men in great need
Caring, warm women
Are a gift to everyone
Including old men
A man's fantasy
A seductive young woman
In his bed with him

The Good Old Days

I was born during Warren G. Harding's administration
—before Lindberg's famous flight,
before the 1929 stock market crash,
before Hoover or FDR became president,
before "talkies," FM radio, long before WW II,
before computers, space travel, and moon landings.
before radar, nylons, air-conditioners,
and electric blankets, and automatic gearshifts —
and before TV, TV dinners, cell phones,
BlackBerrys, Iphones, and x-rated movies.
So, once I was a child.
It was a long time ago, or how would I know:
Of trolley cars and later, trackless trolleys?
Of mailmen who walked their routes
twice every day?
Of cars with running boards and rumble seats?
Of ice wagons pulled by horses?
Of telephones that shared four-party lines.
with live operators who asked.
"Number please?"
Of coal furnaces, coal bins, and coal hods?
Of ice boxes with drip pans that had to be emptied daily?
Of the outhouse on my grandfather's farm
with its crescent on the door
and Montgomery Ward catalog
hanging therein for toilet paper?
Of young women with hats and veils
and skirts to the floor?
Of young men with fedoras in winter
and skimmers in summer?
Yes, once I was a child.
It was a long time ago,
or how would I remember when:

"Made in Japan" meant cheap junk?
Most wives stayed at home to take care of the kids?
Two career marriages were the exception?
Closets were for clothing, not for "coming out of?"
Gay rights, computer dating, online shopping,
and e-mail were unheard of?
A chip was a small piece of wood.?
Hardware was bought in a store
and consisted of tools, cutlery, locks, nails, screws,
and plumbing and electrical supplies?
Music was played by "big bands' and jazz bands,
and consisted of swing, ballads, country and western,
and jive ("Rock," "Rap," and "Hip Hop" came much later)?
In my youth, AIDS were hospital volunteers.
Grass was something you mowed with a push mower.
Pot was a kitchen utensil used for cooking
(or a porcelain one used for night-time emergencies),
I remember when bread and milk,
were delivered (about 4 a.m.) to your door daily
and some few years later, pastries (cakes, pies, etc.)
were delivered by panel truck.
Ice for the icebox was delivered by truck to patrons
who placed a cardboard sign in a window
with the number of pounds needed displayed at the top –
and brought into the house by the driver
using tongs (with a rubber sheet covering his shoulders and back).
And there were other peddlers,
especially in summer: the fruit and vegetable man,
the farmer with his horse drawn wagon,
the weekly visit of the ragman with his horse and wagon,
or the junk man, who bought newspapers and magazines,
metal of all kinds (but at different values),
and other household items,
with considerable dickering and bargaining.
And let us not forget the garbage man,
arriving in his open smelly truck once weekly
to collect the discarded scraps of meat, bones,

vegetable peels, spoiled food,
and the like, which were taken to his pig farm
out of town for feed.
We were taught to share everything:
chicken pox, mumps, measles, even scarlet fever,
and colds, pinworms, ring worms,
head lice, and, during one terrible period, Polio,
When I reached manhood, most couples got married first —
and then lived together,
McDonald's, Pizza Hut, and Burger King did not exist.
Diet drinks and instant coffee were far in the future.
So were Best Buy, Target, Old Navy,
K-Mart, ToysRUs. Radio Shack, and CVS.
I remember, 10–cent trolley fares, dime draught beers
And 10-cent movie matinees.
Lastly, I remember with longing the $650 new car sticker price
12 oz Coke 5c
Large candy bar (Milky Way, Three Musketeers,
Hershey's Milk Chocolate) 5c
Roller coaster or other carnival ride 10c
Pint of Fried clams 25c
Ice cream cone double scoop 5c
McCann's banana split w/ 3 scoops
(vanilla, chocolate, and strawberry),
sliced banana, crushed nuts, and whipped cream 10c
Yes, those were the good old days!

Something Worthwhile

Do something today that tomorrow
will prove to be really worthwhile.
Help me to conquer sorrow
and greet each day with a smile.
For only through kindness and giving
of service and friendship and cheer,
Do we learn the pure joy of living
and find heaven's happiness here.

On Being a Dad

Dads don't have it easy
They seldom know how to relate to others,
particularly their older daughters,
because they grew up not understanding how to show love.

When their daughters were between five and ten,
it was so easy and natural to hug and kiss them,
to hold them in their lap, to sweet-talk their little girls,
the diminutive people they could feel close to,
the tiny women who loved them unconditionally.

But when their daughters grow up,
instead of overtly showing affection,
most dads resort to giving advice.
They equate advice giving with expressing love.

So, listen to your dad. You don't have to follow his advice,
just pay attention and tell him that you will think about
what he has suggested.
He is only trying to show you that he cares.
And always remember that Dad misses the little lass
who used to be his little girl, his Pigeon, his Peanut,
and that he loves you more than you can imagine.

Aphorisms

Dads don't have it easy
They don't know how to relate
But they love anyway
Love is not earned
It's given by another
Accept it "as is"

Totem Pole Ballroom, Norumbega Park

Opened in June 1897, in the Auburndale section
of Newton, Massachusetts
It was one of the many "trolley parks" of the era,
popular with the middle class urban population
who sought interesting, fun and affordable recreation.

In 1930, Norumbega's Great Steel Theater
was converted into the Totem Pole Ballroom.
From opening day, the Totem Pole was something special.
Although more than a hundred ballrooms
were advertising in the Boston newspapers,
the Totem Pole was acknowledged by all
as the best and the most elegant in all creation.
It was "the utmost in refinement –
Couples only, and soft drinks exclusively served."
It was America's most beautiful ballroom.

Young lovers danced the night away at the Totem Pole,
to the music of one of the most famous swing bands of the day.
Artie Shaw, Benny Goodman, Lawrence Welk,
Harry James, and Jimmy and Tommy Dorsey.
Or listening to the country's most celebrated entertainers:
Dinah Shore, Frank Sinatra. Ozzie Nelson,
The Four Lads, Frankie Lane, and the Von Trapp Family.
Music from the ballroom was nationally broadcast
over the ABC, CBS, and NBC radio networks.

Patrons paused only to flirt and cuddle
in the ballroom's romantic surroundings
Or sought even more privacy
In the Park's cozy nooks and lush gardens
— or spending intermission in canoes and pedal boats
— on the star-lit Charles River.

I discovered the blandishments of the affordable
Totem Pole and Norumbega Park in1939:
Love seats with high backs and sides
in a half circle around the dance floor,
Providing almost complete privacy.
Low lighting, a revolving crystal ball
sending rays of light to the dancers below,
creating a mystical and romantic atmosphere.

I visited the Totem Pole almost weekly
(except for other weekends at Kimball's Starlight,
Whalom Park, and Canobie Lake ballrooms
during the summer and fall of '39, '40. and '41,
sequentially with Mary, Jean, Lucille, and Kathleen,
my girl friends during that span of time.
They were some of the very best times of my life.

Dancing Haiku

We should slow dance now
To Johnny Mathis' Misty
And enjoy the best

Holding you closely
Is the thing I longed to do
Please let it come true.

You granted my wish
And made my day and my night
Now I am content

Yesterday is gone.
Tomorrow may never come.
Dance the night away

To My Family and Friends

When I am gone, just let me depart,
so I can ease into my new life apart.
You must not dishearten me with your tears;
instead be joyful that we had so many years.
I gave you my love, and you can never guess
how much you gave me true happiness.
I thank you for the love you have shown,
but now it's required that I travel alone.
So, mourn for me a little while if you must
Then let your grief be comforted with trust,
for it's only a short time that we must be apart,
so cherish the memories within your heart.
Rejoice and celebrate my life with me
for it was a life filled with blessings aplenty:
A mother who loved me enough
to give me to her sister Josephine
to rear me as her own son
and ensure that I earned a college degree,
an accomplishment that she admired and revered.
A life partner and wife.
beautiful, supportive, loving, and forgiving,
the greatest gift of the first 75 years of my life.
Six beautiful, healthy, talented, and loving children
twelve wonderful grandchildren, and, to date,
two great grandchildren all matchless flowers
in my exceptional and very private garden and dower.
And, in the late winter of my life,
the beneficence of a very special and loving woman
to give me the companionship, comfort,
and affection I needed when I needed it most,.
And finally, when you must join me alone,
I hope to greet you with a smile, a hug,
and a heartfelt Welcome Home!

Bits and Pieces of Haiku

A happy woman
Is a perfect complement
To a man like me

A lovely woman
Is the ideal solution
For a lonely man

You mean everything
To me in my senior years
So please indulge me.

You are my lifeline
That is something I know well.
Please stay with me now.

Why do I do this?
Don't have the right to love you.
But, I really do!

A lovely woman
Always a work of God's art
Let us be thankful

A burdensome man
An extremely needy guy
with a sincere heart
A special woman
wearing a beguiling smile
and upbeat outlook
The ultimate test
A championship tennis match
Both players winners

Wanting to live long.
To enjoy an interval
Of real happiness.

You are my best friend..
Don't underrate that status.
It's too important.

I'll love you forever
Never reject that truth.
That's the way it has to be .

Living alone sucks.
What can be done about it?
Find a companion

Life is beautiful
Death is irrevocable
Which one do you choose?

When you care for her
You also care about her
— Inseparable

Becky is comely
She epitomizes grace
And true affection

Past the three-point line
Aiming and launching the sphere
Yield: nothing but net

Major league baseball
The American pastime
And my field of dreams

Index

Happy hour habit
A very dry Martini
Nectar of the Gods